LUFTWAFFE AT WAR

German Bombers over England 1940–1944

Crewmen of KG 54 at Coulommiers in France in summer 1940. After early missions over the North Sea and the English Channel *Luftwaffe* crews were trained in anti-shipping operations, in order to mount ship-hunting raids along the sea approaches to the main harbours of England's south and east coasts. Crews were also taught to release their aerial mines in the vicinity of these important targets.

LUFTWAFFE AT WAR

German Bombers over England 1940–1944

Manfred Griehl

Pen & Sword
AVIATION

German Bombers over England

A Greenhill Book
First published in 1999 by Greenhill Books,
Lionel Leventhal Limited
www.greenhillbooks.com

This edition published in 2016 by
PEN & SWORD AVIATION
An imprint of
Pen & Sword Books Ltd
47 Church Street
Barnsley
South Yorkshire
S70 2AS

CIP data records for this title are available from
the British Library

Designed by DAG Publications Ltd
Design by David Gibbons
Layout by Anthony A. Evans

Printed and bound in Malta by Gutenberg Press Ltd

Pen & Sword Books Ltd incorporates the Imprints
of Aviation, Atlas, Family History, Fiction, Maritime,
Military, Discovery, Politics, History, Archaeology,
Select, Wharncliffe Local History, Wharncliffe True
Crime, Military Classics, Wharncliffe Transport,
Leo Cooper, The Praetorian Press, Remember When,
Seaforth Publishing and Frontline Publishing.

For a complete list of Pen & Sword titles
please contact
PEN & SWORD BOOKS LIMITED
47 Church Street, Barnsley, South Yorkshire,
S70 2AS, England
E-mail: enquiries@pen-and-sword.co.uk
Website: www.pen-and-sword.co.uk

LUFTWAFFE AT WAR
GERMAN BOMBERS OVER ENGLAND, 1940–1944

Following the evacuation of the British Expeditionary Force at Dunkirk, the *Luftwaffe* continued to work in close co-operation with the *Wehrmacht* as it advanced towards Paris, which was occupied on 14 June 1940. A few days later, on the 25th, the war against France ended in victory for Germany. The whole campaign had lasted only a few weeks. Many *Luftwaffe* units were then withdrawn to rest and refit in preparation for the next phase of the conflict, which would theoretically complete Germany's conquest of Western Europe — the invasion of Britain. Reinforcements were sent to the German front-line units, the *Luftwaffe* receiving additional medium bombers as well as improved fighter and destroyer aircraft.

Unlike the Royal Air Force's Bomber Command, the *Luftwaffe*'s *Kampfgeschwader* (Bomber Wings) concentrated less on long-range strategic bombing and more on providing direct support to German ground forces. Successful campaigns in Poland, Norway and France had proved the effectiveness of this kind of warfare in the opening stages of the war. By utilising its Stuka dive-bombers and single-engined fighter-bombers to their greatest potential, the *Luftwaffe* established its huge close-support force as the most important element in its air war doctrine.

The downfall of German air power began with the preparations for Operation 'Sea Lion', the projected invasion of Great Britain. It was thought that three months of good weather would prove sufficient to mount an overwhelming air offensive, especially against Southern England and the Midlands. This was to be carried out by *Luftflotten* (Air Fleets) 2 and 3. *Luftflotte* 2 — based in north-east France and the Low Countries, with its headquarters at Brussels — comprised I, II and IX *Fliegerkorps* (Air Corps), while *Luftflotte* 3 — with its headquarters in Paris and its squadrons spread over north-west France — operated IV, V and VIII *Fliegerkorps*. As many as 1,200 bomber aircraft had been assembled for this

new offensive, most of them Do 17Zs and He 111Hs. In addition each *Luftflotte* had numerous single- and twin-engined fighter units at its disposal, equipped with Bf 109s and Bf 110s. Though subordinated to the command of a *Luftflotte* officer called the *Jagdführer* (Fighter Leader, often shortened to *Jafü*), these units nevertheless retained a measure of independence in the choice of when and where they engaged the RAF's fighters. The *Jafü* 2 (*ie* the *Jagdführer* of *Luftflotte* 2) had access to some 460 Bf 109s and 90 Bf 110 destroyer aircraft, while the *Jafü* 3 had over 300 single-engined day fighters and more than 120 Bf 110Cs and Ds.

A further 130 He 111 bombers and additional long-range reconnaissance aircraft belonging to X *Fliegerkorps* (part of *Luftflotte* 5), based in Norway, were also to participate in the operation, as were some 280 Ju 87B Stuka dive-bombers, which were assigned to attack Allied shipping in the English Channel and along the South Coast, as well as RAF coastal airfields and radar installations. It was also believed that the Stukas would prove effective against commercial shipping both on the Thames and in the Hull area.

The OKL (*Oberkommando der Luftwaffe*, or *Luftwaffe* High Command), under Hermann Göring, was set two tasks in Operation 'Sea Lion': firstly, to defeat the Royal Air Force by means of a massive aerial offensive, eliminating its entire fighter force, together with all major ground installations and command posts; and secondly, to strangle Britain's maritime supply lines by attacking its ports and shipping. During the first phase of the offensive it was proposed to destroy all the RAF fighter bases located south of a line between London and Gloucester. Only after this had been achieved would attacks be commenced against those Fighter Command units stationed further north. Additional units would meanwhile launch day and night bombing raids directed against the British aviation and aircraft engine industries, to prevent replacement aircraft from entering service with front-line units. The OKL believed that it could achieve these objectives by means of massive, well-protected bomber raids, escorted by lots of single- and twin-engined fighters.

On 25 June the *Luftwaffe* opened its offensive by a series of attacks designed to test the response times of fighter and anti-aircraft units in every part of Britain. Over the next few days twin-engined *Luftwaffe* bombers began to appear over Britain in considerable numbers, though most of the attacks aimed at individual RAF fighter installations were mounted by no more than about eight to twelve He 111s, escorted by some thirty Bf 109 fighters. In addition up to eighty Ju 87B dive-bombers were employed in raids on shipping and port facilities, and British convoys off the Isle of Wight were also attacked. During these operations the RAF's well-organised air defence system enabled them to shoot down several German aircraft.

Early in August 1940 the *Luftwaffe* launched its first full-scale assault. Escorted by 1,000 day fighters, some 500 bombers of *Luftflotten* 2 and 3 took off to destroy Fighter Command's ground installations. Simultaneous attacks were also mounted by Ju 87 dive-bombers against major targets along the Channel coast, in order to put the ports out of action. However, despite suffering heavy losses, leading to sometimes critical shortages of pilots and aircraft, the RAF's Fighter Command remained operational throughout the assault.

On the night of 25 August RAF bombers appeared over Germany for the first time. Their attacks on Berlin and other targets prompted Adolf Hitler to declare a campaign of revenge attacks against London and other British towns. Consequently on 7 September German bombers were sent against the docks in London's East End, and the following night a further 255 bombers attacked the same area, where huge fires illuminated the target.

However, as the intensity of the raids escalated it became apparent that the German commanders had failed to adequately co-ordinate the activities of their fighters and bombers, with the result that the latter, lacking close air protection, soon began to suffer considerable losses over Great Britain. Between 7 and 15 September 1940 more than 190 heavy bombers and nearly 100 fighters and destroyers failed to return from raids, or were damaged seriously enough that they crashed during the trip back to France or whilst attempting to land at their home bases. The *Luftwaffe*'s leaders had believed that all of the RAF's fighters were based in the south of England, and that they could thus be worn down by constant attacks, and had not realised that

there were additional squadrons in the North which could be rotated south to replace units in need of rest and re-equipping. As it became apparent that the RAF had access to a supply of seemingly 'fresh' first-line fighter squadrons, however, the OKL became convinced that it was impossible to defeat the enemy in this way. Though the German attack was nevertheless maintained, albeit on a smaller scale, by a force comprising some thirty Ju 88A-1s together with 200 German fighters, it became increasingly obvious that the continual drain on its operational strength would eventually reduce the *Luftwaffe*'s offensive potential to a critical level.

During the weeks that followed, a deterioration in the weather was believed to be responsible for the cancellation of daylight operations over Britain. *Luftwaffe* crews nevertheless carried out several raids against British heavy industry by night, without fighter protection, but these were too small to stand any chance of damaging the enemy sufficiently to enable Operation 'Sea Lion' to be mounted.

The fundamental weakness in Germany's air strategy lay in the deficiency of its fighter arm rather than in its powerful force of dive-bombers and heavy bombers. The defensive armament of the *Luftwaffe*'s Do 17, He 111 and Ju 88 bombers was insufficient — on its own — to protect them against heavy RAF fighter attacks, so they had to rely instead on fighter escorts; and the frequent absence of these in moments of crisis led to many losses. Furthermore, the OKL and, especially, its intelligence department, did not know enough about the British 'early warning' radar system, based along the coast. Nor were they aware of the RAF's sophisticated ground control system, which could vector defending fighters towards an incoming bomber force by means of ground-to-air radio communications. This enabled the British to employ those fighter squadrons best placed to attack (*ie* those nearest to, or lying in the path of, the approaching raid), and enabled them to commit only as many aircraft as were needed to counter the perceived threat. The rest could then be held back as a reserve. Only on those occasions when there were no German escort fighters present were large concentrations of RAF fighters assembled in any one sector.

There were also other flaws in the *Luftwaffe*'s strategy. It had already become obvious during the campaign in France, for instance, that Spitfire and Hurricane fighters were well armed, with up to eight machine-guns in their wings, and their combat performance was an important factor which, combined with the British fighter control and plotting systems, contributed to saving many RAF pilots and aircraft during the height of the Battle of Britain (August to September 1940). Widely dispersed anti-aircraft formations and balloon barrages also served to disrupt German raids, as, in no small way, did the Observer Corps, a network of civilian-manned posts which plotted and reported the path of enemy aircraft passing overhead.

The operational shortcomings of the twin-engined *Zerstörer* (destroyer) aircraft, the Bf 110, was another factor in the failure of the *Luftwaffe*'s campaign. This long-range escort fighter was found to need its own escort of single-seat Bf 109s to beat off attacks by Hurricanes and Spitfires, which left the short-range 109s as the only available escort fighters. However, because drop-tanks had not yet been developed these could only carry sufficient fuel to stay with the bombers for a few minutes once they were over London. Operating further afield, such as over the Midlands, the He 111s could not rely on having escorts at all and could only operate by night if they were to stand any chance of success. Thus, by October 1940, the *Luftwaffe* was obliged to alter its strategy, and began instead to throw the weight of its bombing effort into night attacks against London. Its aim now was to reduce the morale of the British people and destroy their war economy by demolishing the capital. However, switching the main emphasis of its bombing offen-sive to London left the *Luftwaffe* with insufficient aircraft to raid ports and harbour installations else-where in Britain, or to lay mines in the English Channel and along other important shipping lanes.

October saw fewer German bombers shot down, but many more were damaged. In addition large numbers were grounded by a lack of replacement parts, which resulted from the excessive demands of keeping aircraft operational when several at a time might return from a raid suffering from severe combat damage. This led to a reduction in the num-ber of aircraft available for the German offensive and gave the British air defence a breathing space to refit and increase its own numerical strength.

For the *Luftwaffe*, the switch to night bombing immediately brought with it the additional prob-lems of navigating and bomb-aiming in the dark. It was believed that the radio-guidance beams known as 'Knickebein' and 'X' would allow for precision navigation and the bombing of targets in darkness, but there were too many complications for bombs to be dropped on a small target with guaranteed accuracy. Another problem introduced by night-fly-ing was that more He 111s and other aircraft were damaged landing back at their airfields in the dark than were actually lost in combat. Despite the trans-

fer of ninety new aircraft to their front-line units, the offensive potential of *Luftflotten* 2, 3 and 5 was reduced from 1,300 bombers to an effective strength of only 700 twin-engined aircraft during this phase of the Blitz, and of these only some fifty per cent were usually serviceable.

The night attacks were sometimes organised on a grand scale — on 9 October 1940, for instance, a total of 487 bombers carrying some 400,000 kg of bombs, including 70,000 incendiaries, appeared over London — but on some nights the strength of the raiders was reduced to between just 150 and 300 bombers. It was thus found impossible to effect the level of destruction sought by the German lead-ership. The poor results achieved by these attacks on industrial targets, coupled with the fact that civilian morale had not collapsed under aerial bom-bardment, led to Göring's staff to introduce yet another change in their strategy, after informing the *Reichsmarschall* that it was impossible to subdue the enemy within the next month — the final dead-line if 'Sea Lion' was to be launched in 1940. Noc-turnal attacks against targets all over London by a reduced force of 100 to 150 twin-engined bombers were to continue with the help of the 'Knickebein' navigation system, but in addition daylight mis-sions were to be mounted by single-engined fighter-bombers. Special forces operating a few Do 217s were despatched to destroy key elements of the British armaments industry, while the remaining forces of *Luftflotten* 2 and 3 combined to obliterate the industrial cities of Birmingham, Coventry and Liverpool. Because it was found that SC 50 bombs (50 kg high explosives) did not inflict sufficient damage, the German high command ordered that their bombers should be loaded instead with the heaviest GP (general purpose) bombs and all kinds of incendiary devices, from large liquid incendiaries down to 1 kg bombs. IX *Fliegerkorps* was meanwhile ordered to concentrate on minelaying operations over the Thames, as well as along the Bristol Chan-nel, the Mersey, and the Manchester Ship Canal. Fur-thermore it was ordered to destroy the Rolls-Royce factory and to interdict shipping in the English Channel and the Thames.

The year closed with a massive air raid against London on the evening of 29 December, when extensive fires were started after the *Pfadfinder-Bomber* (Pathfinders) had placed their incendiary marker-bombs squarely on target.

During the early part of 1941 the Germans bombed the main British ports, especially Bristol, Cardiff, Hull, Plymouth and Swansea. In April, how-ever, some bomber squadrons were withdrawn from their bases in northern France for service in the Balkan campaign. On only one occasion thereafter, on 10 May 1941, was the *Luftwaffe* able to muster enough aircraft to mount a large-scale attack on London, when some 550 bombers dropped a total of 700,000 kg of GP bombs, including 86,000 incendiaries. During the next month only small raiding forces appeared over Britain, and after Hitler had launched his invasion of Russia in June 1941 the only *Luftwaffe* bomber squadrons left in the West were elements of KG (*Kampfgeschwader*, or Bomber Wings) 2, 26 and 30, specifically to continue anti-shipping raids and minelaying operations around Britain's coasts. The *Fliegerführer Atlantik*, who was responsible for aerial operations over the Bay of Biscay and parts of the Atlantic up to the Irish Sea, had no more than 155 combat aircraft at his disposal, these forces being insufficient to achieve any noteworthy success.

During 1941 and 1942 only limited raids were mounted against England. Bf 109s carried out low-level cross-Channel raids on coastal targets, and small numbers of bombers were sometimes despatched to attack important specific targets. In October 1942 Fw 190 fighter-bombers, followed by a large force of night bombers, attacked Canterbury. Further minor raids were flown by the pilots of SKG 10 (SKG standing for *Schnellkampfgeschwader*, literally Fast Bomber Wing, or Fighter-Bomber Wing), which was equipped with the Fw 190A. Early in 1943 a new staff position, the *Angriffsführer England* (England Attack Command), was established by the OKL, which concentrated the fighter-bombers of SKG 10 and the Me 410s and Do 217s of KG 2 under the command of Oberst Dietrich Peltz.

Because Britain had meanwhile succeeded in enlarging its radar network and setting up a sophisticated defensive system utilising well-armed nightfighters, German nocturnal raids became steadily more costly after 1942. More and more Beaufighters, Defiants, Havocs and Mosquitos had become available to interdict German aerial operations. In March 1943 alone KG 2 lost twenty-six complete crews during offensive operations over Britain and minelaying duties at sea. Nevertheless, despite such losses KG 6 and KG 66 were repeatedly able to penetrate England's air defences with small forces of Do 217s, He 111s and Ju 88s to bomb key industrial targets.

Between December 1943 and March 1945 a final series of air raids against Britain were mounted by Peltz, now a Generalmajor. Amongst the attacking aircraft for the first time were the huge, four-engined He 177A-3 bombers of I/KG 100 (I *Gruppe* of *Kampfgeschwader* 100) carrying SC 2500 (2,500

kg) bombs, of which only a very limited number were available. SC 1800 and SC 1500 bombs were also accommodated in the He 177's bomb-bays. The Do 217s and Ju 188s of KG 2 and the Ju 88s belonging to KG 76, meanwhile, were fitted with the large AB 1000 (AB standing for *Abwurfbehälter* or weapons container) filled with small bomblets, mostly incendiaries. In addition to these *Kampfgeschwader*, elements of KG 30, 40 and 54, together with the Fw 190s of I/SKG 10, were engaged in this offensive, which commenced on the afternoon of 21 January 1944, when 462 out of the 524 bombers available were reported to be serviceable. A total of 732 bombers took part in three attacks mounted by IX *Fliegerkorps* on 21, 22 and 30 January, though engine failures and other faults, especially amongst the Ju 188s and He 177s, as well as the Ju 88s and Do 217s, led to as many as 101 aircraft having to abort before reaching their targets. Others were hit by RAF nightfighters.

Germany's limited offensive potential by this stage of the war necessitated its use of low-cost flying bombs and other 'secret weapons'. By 26 July 1944 as many as 691,000 houses in Britain had been hit or damaged by German V1 rocket bombs, even though a lot of these missiles had either malfunctioned en route or had been shot down by anti-aircraft batteries or RAF fighters, especially Spitfire Mk XIVs, during their approach. The use of air-launched V1s was stopped in 1945 due to the large number of casualties amongst, and the lack of fuel for, the He 111H bombers which carried and launched them above the North Sea. On 8 September 1944, however, the first of the next generation of longer-range missiles, called V2s, hit Chiswick in west London, killing three people and wounding ten. By the end of the war the German *Vergeltungswaffen* or 'revenge weapons', as the V1 and V2 were known, had between them been responsible for killing 8,938 people in Britain and wounding 24,234, as well as destroying some 28,000 houses and damaging more than a million others, despite the failure of every fifth missile fired. The last unmanned V-weapon launched against Britain exploded on 27 March 1945. After that the remaining V1s and V2s were directed against alternative targets, especially the Belgian supply ports being used by the Allies.

Continuous pressure from Allied ground forces had by now forced the Germans into a steady retreat, as a result of which airfields that would have enabled them to launch jet bomber attacks against Britain were lost, along with any further hope of countering the final enemy advance into Germany in 1945.

A well-armed Do 17Z of 9/KG 76, boasting eight MG 15 guns protruding from its so-called 'glasshouse' canopy when most such aircraft had only six. The mechanic in the cockpit is overseeing the running of the engines prior to the aircraft taking off for its next combat mission.

Do 17Z bombers belonging to KG 2 (as indicated by the fuselage code 'U5' visible to the left of the cross on the nearest machine) en route to Britain. After crossing the English Channel, Dornier pilots often tried to reach their targets by flying at low level.

Above: Two 'black men' (the *Luftwaffe* nickname for ground-crew, from the colour of their overalls) installing an MG FF 20 mm gun in the nose of a He 111H-4, after the fire-power of MG 15 machine-guns had proved insufficient to destroy ground targets.

Below: An early conversion of a He 111H-6 bomber capable of carrying two of the large SC 1000 or SC 1800 bombs beneath its fuselage, which rendered it impossible to load bombs in the aircraft's internal bomb-bays. Note the bomb hooks just visible under the wing root.

A He 111H of KG 26 (known as the *Löwengeschwader*, or 'Lion Group') is prepared for its next mission over Western Europe. The aircraft shown is one of the early H models which could only carry eight SC 250 bombs internally, these being held vertically in their racks in two rows of four, one to each side of the fuselage central walkway.

This He 111P (B3+BL) belonging to 3/KG 54 crashed at Cambrai in France during the summer of 1940 after being hit by enemy fire. One crew member was killed.

A He 111 warming-up in France during the winter of 1940–1. The number of German air raids launched at this time was rather small as a result of the preparations being made for both the campaign in the Balkans and the invasion of Russia.

Above: A combat formation of Do 217E-4s over France. In order to avoid being attacked by their own anti-aircraft formations *Luftwaffe* units were ordered to identify their aircraft by means of coloured stripes, such as those seen on these Dorniers. Despite this, however, new combat aircraft were frequently fired on by *Luftwaffe* Flak units, especially in occupied countries which were regularly subjected to RAF attacks.

Below: A Fw 200C long-range combat aircraft, used to support German U-boat raids and to provide air escort for the submarines as they returned home. Some crews succeeded in sinking British merchant vessels far out into the Atlantic.

This Fw 200C is being prepared for its next mission. Several of these four-engined aircraft were shot down by RAF fighters or by anti-aircraft fire put up by the ships being attacked.

Four pages of reconnaissance photographs from the *Reichsluftfahrtministerium*'s '*Seehafenatlas Grossbritannien*', a two-volume ring-bound atlas comprising maps and photographs of 132 British ports, docks and harbours. Maps contained details of harbour size and capacity, with any extra observations that might prove useful. Classified '*geheim*' ('secret'), the atlas also set down criteria for judging the significance of harbours, and noted general points relevant for attacks from the air. (*Leventhal Collection*) **Above:** Lowestoft harbour. **Below:** Newhaven harbour.

Newhaven

Maßstab etwa 1:15 000

0   100   200   300   400   500   1000m

Lowestoft

Maßstab etwa 1:13 500

0   100   200   300   400   500   1000m

Folkestone

Maßstab etwa 1:16 700

0   100   200 300 400 500   1000 m

Above: An early Do 17Z belonging to KG 76 of I *Fliegerkorps*, which was part of *Luftflotte* 2. Because their lack of armour rendered these bombers extremely vulnerable, many of their missions were flown at low level. KG 76 was re-equipped with the more powerful Ju 88A before being transferred to the Eastern Front.

Below: Most of the *Luftwaffe*'s twin-engined bombers received a coat of black camouflage in preparation for night operations, in order to provide them with some protection against British nightfighters and ground fire. The aircraft being painted here is a Do 17Z-2 of KG 76, carrying improved defensive armament consisting of additional machine-guns on both sides of the cabin.

Above: This photograph was taken at Reichenbach, a refuelling stop en route to the Western theatre of war. The He 111H belonged to KG 27, whose staff and I—III *Gruppen* came under the command of IV *Fliegerkorps* of *Luftflotte* 2. The unit, based at Dinard, was later taken over by *Luftflotte* 3 and continued to mount air operations over England.

Below: This He 111H-3 is one of those operated by KG 4, 26 or 28, which were flown by crews serving with *Luftflotte* 3 in Western Europe. Because the early He 111Hs were not equipped with external racks, only bombs which individually weighed no more than 250 kg could be accommodated within the bomb-bay.

Right: An He 111H of KG 4 releases its bombs. The three bombs at the bottom of the photograph have probably been released by another aircraft. The bomb-bays of both the H and P versions of the He 111 could carry a maximum of eight SC 250 bombs (weighing 250 kg each), which were stowed vertically, nose uppermost. Note how quickly the bombs 'tumble'.

Below: During the winter of 1939–40 this He 111P-4 of I/KG 53 provided crew-training by flying long-range missions over Germany. Such training had facilitated the elimination of French, Dutch, and Belgian air power during the early stages of the war, as well as the destruction of many RAF aircraft in preparation for Operation 'Sea Lion', the projected invasion of the British Isles.

Above: Two men of III/KG 53 pose in front one of their He 111H-3s, spring 1940. This particular Heinkel is one of those which served with the early form of defensive armament, which comprised just three or four MG 15 machine-guns. The bomb seems to be an early SC 500 with an old type of fin.

Below: Another He 111H-3 belonging to III/KG 53. Note the three vertical stripes added to its fin for identification during the early phase of day-time raids over Southern England and London.

Right: An He 111H-3 of KGr 100 (KGr standing for *Kampfgruppe*, or Bomber Group) being loaded with air markers, designed to enable the bomber crews which followed the designated *Pfadfinder* (pathfinder) aircraft to find their target by day or night. Specialised armament of this kind was introduced during the late 1930s.

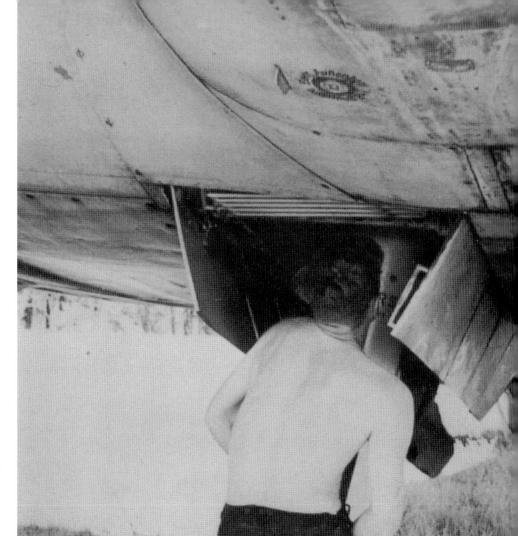

Below: This He 111H-2 (9K+FN), being transferred to a front-line airfield in Western Europe in 1940, was operated by a crew belonging to II/KG 51 'Edelweiss'.

Above: The ground-crew of this He 111H-4 belong to II/KG 26. Alongside a non-commissioned officer of the *Löwengeschwader*, they display their large SC 500 bombs and smaller SC 250s before loading them aboard the twin-engined bomber, the under-surfaces of which are painted black for the *Luftwaffe*'s night offensive over England. Note the messages chalked on the bombs: that on the right translates as 'Greetings to W.C.' (*ie* Winston Churchill).

Right: A small part of the *Luftwaffe*'s bomber force was stationed on the west coast of Norway, including this He 111H of KG 26, armed with an early SC 1000 bomb. During its stay in Norway KG 26 came under the command of X *Fliegerkorps*, November 1940. It was later handed over to I *Fliegerkorps* of *Luftflotte* 3, which was tasked with bombing British targets by night and day. For protection against the elements the aircraft's fuselage is sheathed in thick canvas.

Left: A 'combat box' of eight He 111H-3s and H-4s belonging to 4 *Staffel* of KG 53 (4/KG 53). The aircraft are camouflaged for night raids over Britain.

Right: After the surrender of France a lot of these Renault UE vehicles – designated SdKfz (*Sonderkraft-fahrzeuge*) 630(f) by the Germans – were used by *Luftwaffe* bomber units, to tow heavy bomb loads such as the SC 1800 (or SC 1700) depicted here. The bomb is loaded on a *Transport-gestell* 5, a skid for towing loads across meadows between runways.

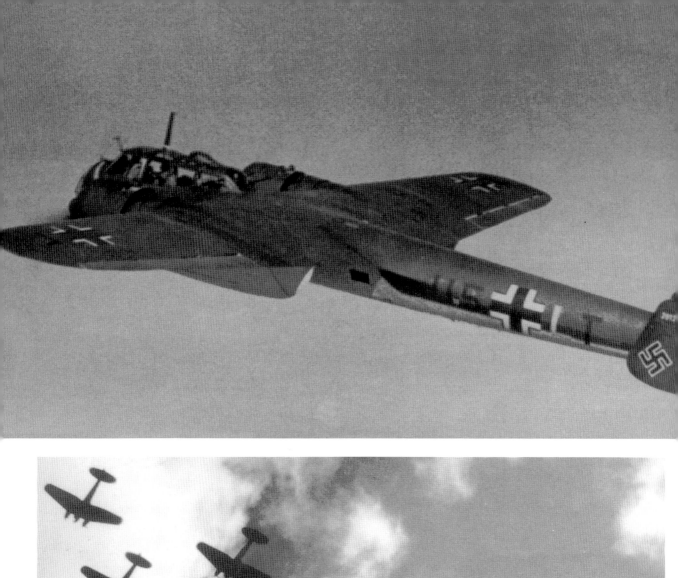

Above: A downed He 111H-6. British fighter pilots were often able to inflict serious losses on attacking bombers because insufficient fuel capacity obliged the German fighter escorts to turn back before the bombers had reached their targets. The firepower of the Hurricane and Spitfire, and even the Defiant, was powerful enough to destroy Do 17s, He 111s and Ju 88s flying without Bf 109s or Bf 110s in close attendance. The escort missions flown by Bf 110 crews were themselves very costly owing to this aircraft's inferior performance.

Above: Do 17Z-2 U5+IT (s/n 2612) belonged to 9/KG 2. It is here seen crossing the North Sea en route to targets along the British coast.

Left: After being provided with ammunition for their guns, loaded up with all kinds of bombs and refuelled with as much aviation gasoline as their tanks could take, formations of KG 26 head out to attack coastal targets, London, or the industrial centres of the Midlands. But without adequate fighter protection these missions proved to be very costly.

Right: This He 111H-3 (V4+FL) of KG 1 'Hindenburg' was hit during a raid over the Midlands in October 1940 but nevertheless made good its escape. It took the ground-crew a long time to install replacement parts and repair the destroyed fuselage panel. This aircraft's swastikas and under-surfaces have been painted black to reduce its chances of being seen either from the ground or by a nightfighter crew.

Above: A mixed formation of He 111H-1s and H-3s belonging to KGr 100, whose crews later participated in a lot of difficult night-time raids utilising the top secret 'X' radio navigation guidance-beam system which was installed in some of their bombers. This photograph was possibly taken on 9 August 1940, when parts of KGr 100 were transferred from Lüneburg to Vannes in western France, to serve as a pathfinder unit alongside other *Luftwaffe* bomber formations.

Below: Two He 111 bombers stand ready for action over the British Isles in autumn 1940. One — an He 111H-3 (6N+EK) of 2 *Staffel* (squadron), KGr 100 — is equipped with an 'X' navigation system (revealed by the extra aerial masts on the fuselage). Note that, as was often the case, the fin section has not been painted black but instead retains its former camouflage. In addition the ventral gun position has been replaced, possibly as a result of combat damage, and is still coloured bright blue rather than black.

Above: These *Luftwaffe* ground-crew are filling the magazines for MG FF aircraft cannon with 20 mm shells and checking the defensive armament. Note the vehicles in the background. Some of the trucks used by KG 53 in western France were former French or Belgian vehicles captured by the *Wehrmacht* during the initial phase of the campaign in Western Europe.

Below: This He 111H-3 (1H+CB) belonged to the *Gruppenstab* (headquarters flight) of I/KG 26. The staff of a component *Kampfgruppe* of a *Geschwader* operated three or more bombers and a few liaison aircraft, often including captured types. The Heinkel bomber was initially armed with three MG 15 machine-guns fixed in what the Germans called the A, B and C positions (respectively nose, dorsal, and ventral locations). Later they were rearmed or were converted into trainers (the He 111H-9 and H-10). Some were finally fitted with an enclosed turret in place of the B-position open hatch.

Left: *Feldwebel* Horst Götz was one of the *Luftwaffe*'s most famous bomber pilots. During his career he flew several types of piston-engined bombers as well as the fast Ar 240s and the more powerful Ar 234 jets. He is pictured here with two crewmen, in front of a He 111H-3 of 1 *Staffel* of KGr 100 in France, 1940. The aircraft still has the standard camouflage common to all German bombers during the opening stages of the Second World War.

Left: Another He 111H-3 (6N+CK), this time belonging to 2 *Staffel* of KGr 100, which was based in western France as a secret pathfinder unit operating the 'X' navigation system. The three antennae along the top of the fuselage resulted in Heinkels equipped with the 'X' system being nicknamed 'three-masters'. The aircraft's worn skin shows that it has survived numerous missions. Because most operational airfields did not have concrete runways heavy tractors were widely used.

Left: The most powerful bombs carried by He 111s consisted of SC 1000s, SC 1700s and SC 1800s. Because most German bombs were sprayed light grey it proved necessary to repaint them black for use at night. *Luftwaffe* personnel, who unofficially took photographs of their bombs, often added their own greetings to the enemy, such as on this SC 1000 L2 destined for England.

Above: One of the first He 111H-6s to be fitted with the 'Y' radio beam guidance system was coded RN+GW. It was tested by the *Erprobungsstelle* (test centres) at Rechlin and Werneuchen and then handed over to KGr 100. The ventral position was now armed with a MG FF cannon firing forwards and a second weapon, normally a MG 15 machine-gun, firing rearwards. Some of these aircraft were also equipped with a fixed MG 17 or a grenade launcher installed in the tail cone.

Below: A black-painted He 111H-4 equipped with 'Y' system navigation, and with one partly-camouflaged SC 1000 bomb hanging beneath the fuselage, revs up in preparation for a raid against Britain. The last motor check before take-off was customarily watched by the pilot. Only the upper part of the aircraft's fuselage, fin and wings were left in conventional splinter camouflage.

Above: Three of the five non-commissioned officers of this crew, posing in front of their He 111H-3 (s/n 3325), have been decorated with the Iron Cross first class. The aircraft's black camouflage has worn away from the leading edge of the engine nacelle and the gun-sight. Below the canopy can be seen KG 100's badge, a Viking boat.

Below: Among the combat aircraft employed against the Royal Navy and British merchant shipping was this Ju 88A-1 of II/KG 30, which saw action in the vicinity of Hull, Bristol, the Thames estuary and along the East Coast. KG 30's diving eagle emblem, visible on the nose, is here painted on a red shield, this colour indicating that the aircraft belonged to the *Geschwader*'s II *Gruppe*. The ventral gun position has been modified to incorporate armour.

Right: This Ju 88A-1 of I/KG 30 was stationed in France during the summer of 1940. That it belongs to an early batch of A-1s can be seen from the fact that its defensive armament is not fitted in a bullet-proof glass rotating mount. The aircraft is operated by a crew of four; the observer is just checking the ignition of the starboard Jumo 211B engine.

Centre right: Another Ju 88A-1 (s/n 5060) which participated in the *Luftwaffe*'s night offensive against Britain, its *Balkenkreuze* (straight-edged crosses on the wings and fuselage), aircraft code and *Hakenkreuz* (swastika on the tail) having been painted out in black. This aircraft was operated by 1 *Staffel* of KG 51 'Edelweiss' and was fitted with two additional MG 15 guns, one each side of the canopy. The wire running along the top of the fuselage from the canopy led to a dinghy, housed in its own compartment.

Right: The Ju 88A-5 followed the A-1, from which it differed in having longer wings, two more powerful piston engines (Jumo 211G-1s) and generally improved equipment. The aircraft depicted has just arrived in northern France to join one of the combat groups based there. Aircraft were not fully armed during the transfer flight from Central Germany to Western Europe.

Above: A huge SC 1800 bomb – an early version fitted with the old style of fin – is manoeuvred beneath a Ju 88A-5 of KG 77 by a Renault UE (Modell 1936R) tankette. The *Sonderkraftfahrzeuge* 630(f), as the Germans called it, proved essential in handling heavy payloads on airstrips which lacked concrete runways.

Below: This Ju 88A-1 (3Z+FH) of 1/KG 77 carries a large drop-tank beneath its fuselage. Its defensive armament has been improved by the installation of a fourth MG 15 in the nose, which was operated by the observer. At the top of the forward fuselage the gun sight can be seen. The aircraft is painted in the standard Ju 88 camouflage of 1940.

Above: A night bomber of KG 77 receiving its deadly payload. Ground-crews worked day and night to maintain an aircraft's systems and to carry out all the necessary checks that helped to ensure its safety during a mission. Every 'black man' knew that the lives of the flight-crew depended on his work and dedication.

Below: One of KG 4's He 111H-4s being loaded with two heavy bombs designed for use against merchant shipping in the English Channel or the Thames estuary. For attacks on warships armour-piercing bombs such as the SD 500 and SD 1000, or PC 500 and PC 1000, were required in order to have any effect. The aircraft's entire 'glasshouse' has been covered by a special canvas to keep the cockpit section clean and dry.

Above: The British merchant navy lost a lot of vessels during the early phase of the *Luftwaffe*'s anti-shipping raids around the British coast. Ju 87 dive-bombers, He 111s and Ju 88s succeeded in sinking several unarmed merchant ships and tankers. As many ships as possible were subsequently provided with machine-guns and light anti-aircraft weapons to defend themselves against air attack, and later still the ships were generally organised into convoys under Royal Navy protection.

Left: An *Unteroffizier* (corporal) of 1/KG 30, decorated with the Iron Cross second class and wearing a pilot's badge, passes a Ju 88A-5 concealed beneath camouflage nets. The emblem of KG 30's 1 *Staffel* depicts Chamberlain's umbrella, representing the heart of England, beneath a targeting sight. Because this aircraft was being used for nocturnal raids all its lower surfaces have been painted black.

Below: This Do 217E-4 (U5+TE, s/n 5471) was operated by crews from III/KG 2. To achieve better results during low-level attacks, many Do 217Es were equipped with a 20 mm MG FF cannon fixed in the aircraft's nose. This was used by the observer, who sat to the right of the pilot. Like most He 111s and Ju 88s, this Do 217 is also painted black to make it less easy to see from the ground at night.

Above: A Do 217E-2 of II/KG 2 'Holzhammer' (Mallet), armed with four forward-firing guns, prepares for its next mission over England. Besides a moveable MG FF cannon, a second 20 mm weapon (an MG 151/20) is fitted in the nose section, while MG 15 machine-guns are installed on each side of the forward part of the cockpit. The crew are putting on their parachutes and checking their personal equipment prior to boarding the aircraft.

Below: A formation of Do 217E-2s of II/KG 2 'Holzhammer' crossing the north-western corner of Europe on their way back from England. The white of their *Balkenkreuze* has been partly painted over in black, to render the aircraft less visible in darkness.

Right: One of II/KG 2's Do 217Es has been hit by British anti-aircraft fire. Its port propeller has been feathered as the crew heads back towards the French coast escorted by another of the *Gruppe*'s Dorniers.

Right: This Do 217E-4 of 5/KG 2 taking off from Gilze-Rijn in Holland is one of the small number of aircraft which, operated by well trained and highly experienced crews, carried out low-level daylight raids over England in 1941. Some of these aircraft had all of their surfaces painted in light blue or grey.

Right: U5+KN of 5/KG 2 was photographed by another crew as it returned home after a raid. Most of the *Luftwaffe*'s attacks were carried out by night or in the early hours in order to minimise losses.

Above: As well as the Do 217Es operated by KG 2, Do 217E-2s and E-4s were also flown by one of KG 40's *Gruppen*. The particular aircraft shown here, photographed somewhere in Belgium or France in late summer 1940, belonged to 6/KG 40, which was subordinated to IX *Fliegerkorps*, part of *Luftflotte* 2. The observer checks the engines' run-up, watched by his pilot.

Opposite page, top: Two Do 217E-4s of 8/KG 2 at Toulouse-Francazal airfield in November 1942. The rear defensive armament consists of an MG 131 gun in an hydraulically-operated turret, plus a couple of MG 15 guns, one on each side of the cockpit canopy. This picture was taken during 8 *Staffel*'s transfer flight. The aircraft are painted with distinguishing stripes round the wings and

the rear fuselage to prevent them from being fired on by their own anti-aircraft units.

Right: Do 217E-4 (U5+KS, s/n 5462) was part of 8/KG 2 '*Holzhammer*' and took part in the famous raid on the Rolls Royce plant at Derby on 27 July 1942. Despite the fact that most E-4s operated at night or during the early hours many were not equipped with flame dampers; consequently they became easy targets for experienced RAF nightfighter pilots.

Below: A pair of Do 214E-4s (U5+FN and U5+RM) belonging to a formation of five aircraft, en route to their target area. U5+FN (s/n 5532) was shot down by an RAF nightfighter near Beaminster in Dorset at 2230 hours on 16 February 1943.

Left: Do 217E-4 (U5+DT, s/n 4263) and several other E-2s and E-4s were scrapped at Schiphol in the Netherlands after being damaged by RAF intruders or crashing as they returned from raids suffering from heavy damage inflicted by anti-aircraft fire or nightfighter attacks. This picture was taken in the summer of 1942.

Left: A few He 111H-3s were modified by the addition of large, cable-cutting fenders designed to protect them against barrage balloon cables. Such aircraft were designated as He 111H-8s. Propelled by Jumo 211 D-1 or F-1 piston engines, they were operated by III/KG 4, II/KG 27 and one of the *Staffeln* belonging to KG 55, all under the command of *Luftflotte* 3. Crews from these units were frequently sent against maritime targets which utilised balloons as a means of protection from low-level attacks.

Left: As well as the He 111H-8, a small number of Ju 88A-5s were also equipped with the cable-cutting outrigger and redesignated as A-6s. Their armament and equipment remained otherwise largely unchanged, though some underwent a reduction in their rear defensive armament in order to save weight. The hinged crew entry hatch can be seen hanging open here, with its ladder folded down.

Above: Two Ju 88A-6s were shot down on 9 June and 26 June 1941 near Broadfields Down and at Cranborne in Dorset. These aircraft were equipped with external bomb racks installed beneath the inner wing sections; part of one of these is just visible at the top of the photograph, between the engine nacelle (left) and the fuselage (right).

Below: Two aircraft belonging to II/KG 2, based at Deelen in the Netherlands, photographed early in 1943. Both are Do 217K-1s, which have been re-armed with MG 81 Zs in place of the old MG 15, the latter having proved ineffective against enemy fighter aircraft. To minimise the risk of serious damage during low-level attacks by RAF intruders the unit has dispersed its aircraft across the whole airfield.

Opposite page, top: A close-up view of a Do 217K-1 (s/n 4439) of III/KG 2 'Holzhammer'. This is clearly a new aircraft which has just arrived at one of the *Geschwader*'s airfields, since it still lacks its defensive armament. The amended canopy, with its better cockpit layout and improved instrumentation, enhanced the Do 217's operational performance. Despite these improvements, however, many still fell victim to Britain's strengthened night-time defences.

Opposite page, bottom: This Do 217K-1 (U5+RC) was part of 7/KG 2 and operated over southern England, London and the Midlands early in 1943. The *Kutonase*, an anti-barrage balloon cable-cutting device, is partially visible.

Above: A Do 217K-1 (s/n 4446) of KG 2, fitted with an effective flame damping system over its exhausts. Its fuselage is spattered with mud as a result of the unit having to disperse its aircraft in shelters hidden amongst the woods and farms surrounding the airfield, to prevent them being seen by RAF reconnaissance aircraft. This meant in turn that they had to be towed to and from the runway by means of small field paths.

Below: Shortly before taking off for its next bombing raid this Do 217K-1 (U5+EN, s/n 4479) of 5/KG 2 is having SC 250 bombs loaded into its bomb-bay. Note the large *Balkenkreuz*, which, unusually, has not been painted over in black. The figure to the left of the main landing gear is the *Spiess*, a senior NCO responsible for discipline within the squadron.

Above: This ground-crew belonging to II/KG 2 is working on a BMW 801 MA-2 double radial engine inside a hangar. Frequently essential work had to be carried out in the open air without any protection against the elements, even during bad or cold weather. Note the use of an SC 250 bomb's transportation box as a platform by the engineer working beneath the nacelle.

Left: A Do 217E-4 (s/n 5453) of KG 2 '*Holzhammer*' being loaded with aerial mines of LMB type, used to hamper shipping routes along Britain's coasts and estuaries. Because minelaying missions did not involve any low-level flying both the MG FF and the MG 151/20 have been removed from the aircraft's nose.

Above: A He 111H-4 belonging to the *Gruppenstab* of KG 26 waits for two LMA aerial mines, resting on small trolleys in the foreground, to be loaded. As was frequently the case when Do 217s and Ju 88s were employed for minelaying missions, the nose armament has been removed. However, the rearward-facing weapons were retained for defence against nightfighters. British bomb disposal experts were able to disarm an LMA mine and discover the secrets of its fuse arrangement, thereby allowing them to develop and introduce effective countermeasures.

Below: Nine Do 217K-1s from a *Staffel* belonging to II/KG 2. This picture was taken during one of the raids which made up Operation 'Steinbock' in early 1944.

Above: The aircraft of KG 40 were used to attack the merchant vessels which, by transporting vital supplies, enabled the British to maintain their struggle against Germany and keep the population fed. This Fw 200C-3 of III/KG 40 belongs to the forces allocated to the *Fliegerführer Atlantik*, under the command of *Luftflotte* 3. It flew such anti-shipping missions until 1943.

Below: A close-up view of a Fw 200C-3 (SG+KU, s/n 0045) belonging to I/KG 40. The aircraft of this formation were equipped with two PVL 1006 L individual bomb-racks under each wing. This particular aircraft eventually crashed near Rochefort on 2 November 1941 and was destroyed.

Above: During the period when Allied merchant ships sailed singly or in small groups it proved easy to destroy them from the air. However, as the war progressed the Royal Navy introduced a convoy system, in which the merchant vessels were protected by escorts consisting of destroyers and frigates, and sometimes even an auxiliary or 'pocket' aircraft carrier. This dramatically reduced the chances of *Luftwaffe* crews sinking a ship.

Right: From the markings on the tail of their Fw 200C-3 (F8+BT) of III/KG 40, it is apparent that this crew has achieved two air victories and taken part in thirteen combat missions, four of them during the campaign against the British Isles. Because of the Fw 200's weak operational performance, however, its crews had the odds stacked against them in the event of a confrontation with fighters of RAF Coastal Command.

Above: This Ju 88A-14 is one of those handed over to III/KG 54 at Ingolstadt in Bavaria, which were transferred to the Western European theatre at the end of 1943. The aircraft were armed with a 20 mm MG FF cannon in the nose and an additional MG 15 in the cockpit canopy. KG 54's large skull-and-crossbones badge can be seen painted on the side of the fuselage. This unit became a so-called *Kampfgeschwader (Jagd)* when it was equipped with Me 262 jet fighters towards the end of the war.

Below: One of the Ju 88A-4s of KG 54, which had formerly been an A-6 when it was fitted with the large cable-cutting device seen in the earlier photographs. The attachment points for this device can be seen on both sides of the nose glazing. The aircraft is being directed to its dispersal pen near the runway by a member of the ground-crew. It is believed to be one of the bombers sent from Bavaria to support the next phase of attacks against Britain.

Above: This is one of the BM (*Bombenmine*) 1000 mines, code-named 'Monika', which were deployed against Britain. They belonged to a category of bomb which could contain 600 kg of explosives and were fitted with special fuses to prevent them being disarmed by British specialists. The BM 1000 was dropped either by parachute or, fitted with a metal fin section, like a conventional bomb. Note the slogan painted on it: 'An Extra Havana [cigar] for Churchill'.

Above right: This captured French bus was used by a *Feldwerft-Abteilung* (field workshop unit) to test Jumo 211 piston engines. Workshop units were responsible for servicing certain kinds of aircraft and for mechanical tasks believed to be too complex for bomber squadron ground-crews to cope with.

Right: It was difficult for ground-crews to service their aircraft in the open air, but it had to be done. The exhaust system of this piston engine belonging to an aircraft of KG 51 '*Edelweiss*' has been removed prior to replacing the complete engine.

Above: The crew of this Ju 88A-5 of 2/KG 77 succeeded in making a crash landing on the Belgian coast after their aircraft was attacked by RAF nightfighters following a raid on London. Normally crashed aircraft were recovered by special *Luftwaffe* units, but it was not possible to do so in this instance on account of the deep sand. Various instruments and the communication system have nevertheless been salvaged to provide replacement parts for other damaged aircraft.

Below: Because a steady increase in the number of British nightfighters progressively reduced the chances of *Luftwaffe* bombers returning safely to base, the German High Command developed a new tactic. This involved despatching Fw 190A long-range fighter bombers, known as 'Jabo-Reis', against targets in Southern England, each carrying one SC 250 or SC 500 bomb and two 300-litre drop tanks. SKG (*Schnellkampfgeschwader*) 10, which operated these aircraft, was based at St André and Caen from early 1943.

Above: The Fw 190G-3 'Jabo-Rei' had a range of 1,000 to 1,100 km. This picture was taken during the evaluation trials in Germany at the beginning of its career. Only a small number of these fighter bombers ever became available, these becoming part of SKG 10 at an early stage. Of the unit's twenty-two G-3s only sixteen were serviceable and ready for action on 25 December 1943.

Below: This Fw 190G, loaded with two SC 250 bombs, was part of SKG 10, based in France. In autumn 1943 SKG 10's II and III *Gruppen* became II and III/SG 4 (SG standing for *Schlachtgeschwader* or Combat Wing) and were subsequently part of SG 10, which was engaged in the defence of the Normandy coast during the Allied invasion of June 1944. Due to the overwhelming strength of the Allies' forces here there was little chance of achieving more than local successes.

Left: Aircraft of I/KG 66, a German pathfinder unit, were used to destroy important targets at night or during bad weather. In 1944 elements of I *Gruppe* commanded by *Leutnant* Hans Altrogge, flying Ju 88S-3s, reached the City of London and released eighteen marker bombs over Westminster, enabling the main force which followed to bomb the area accurately. Most of KG 66's combat aircraft had well-camouflaged upper surfaces, while the lower surfaces were rendered black.

Left: Side-view of a Ju 88S-1 of KG 6, which came under the command of IX *Fliegerkorps*, part of *Luftflotte* 3. In October 1943 KG 6's squadrons were deployed at bases scattered throughout northern France ready to participate in Operation 'Steinbock', the last *Luftwaffe* air offensive against Great Britain. An impressive number of night bombers were involved in the campaign. During the summer of 1944 KG 6 was ordered to attack advancing Allied ground forces in Normandy.

Left: A Ju 88S-3 of KG 6 taxiing to the runway, powered by Jumo 211 piston engines fitted with flame damping tubes on both side of each nacelle. At the end of 1943 KG 6 consisted of the *Geschwaderstab* (wing headquarters flight) with three bombers, I *Gruppe* with forty-one serviceable aircraft, II *Gruppe* operating thirty-nine, and III *Gruppe* with another forty-one. The unit lost at least eleven Ju 88s during Operation 'Steinbock'.

Left: A Do 217E-2 (Z6+OH) belonging to I/KG 66. This aircraft was stationed at Montdidier in France and flew raids against British targets during late summer 1943. Some of the unit's pathfinders had been equipped with the 'Y' navigation system, which allowed raids to be launched with precision against distant targets. KG 66's Do 217Es remained in early-style camouflage. Because no low-level raids were undertaken an MG 131 was installed in the nose glazing in place of the usual MG FF cannon.

Above: I/KG 66 had been formed during summer 1943 from 15/KG 6 and *Lehr- und Versuchskommando* 17 (Training and Experimental Unit 17, which operated Do 217s), along with *Erprobungskommando* 188 (Ju 188 Experimental Unit), from which a fourth *Staffel* was eventually formed. KG 66 came under the command of IX *Fliegerkorps*. The Do 217E-4 depicted (Z6+FH) was damaged during the return trip from England, when its propeller hit the sea while flying at extremely low level over the Channel.

Left: The 'glasshouse' of another I/KG 66 Do 217K-1 pathfinder. Some Do 217E-4s and K-1s were flown with defensive nose armament consisting of either a twin MG 81 Z or a single MG 131 gun. Three members of the crew can be seen in the roomy interior; the fourth crewman sat ready in the gun-turret at the back of the cabin during take-off and landing, when the aircraft was at its most vulnerable.

Right: A Ju 188A-2 of 4/KG 66. This particular aircraft was armed with two MG 151 guns, of which one was installed in the nose and the other in the turret situated above the cabin. The crew are just pulling on their life-jackets before boarding the aircraft, which is equipped with a *Kutonase* round the forward fuselage, the cabin and the leading edge of both wings. Most Do 217s based in Western Europe were also provided with such cable-cutting devices.

Below: Another Do 217K-1 of KG 66 is prepared for its next mission. Early in 1944 the *Gruppenstab* of KG 66 was based in Montdidier. The unit's 4 *Staffel*, which still flew Ju 188s, was based at St Vannes and moved to Avard in April 1944. The entire wing was later withdrawn to the Antwerpen region of Belgium. The aircraft shown is equipped with the 'Y' navigation system, the antenna for which can be distinctly seen on the cabin roof.

Above: One of the Ju 88S-1s of I/KG 6 crashed at Chievres in June 1943. One crew member may have been injured in this accident, which was caused by the failure of the main landing gear. In order to facilitate rapid evacuation the rear machine-gun was removed from its fairings and the rear part of the cabin jettisoned prior to the emergency landing being attempted.

Below: A Ju 88S-1 belonging to KG 6. This unit was formed from three others: I/KG 6 had formerly been I/KG 77; II/KG 6 was the former *Küstenfliegergruppe* (Coastal Air Group) 106; and III and IV/KG 6 were formed from *Lehrgeschwader* (Training Wing) 1. The unit entered operational service in northern France in October 1943, and flew mainly against targets in Britain.

Right: This test rig for all versions of the Jumo 211 piston engine was built by one of the *Luftwaffe*'s field workshop units during the offensive operations mounted from France in 1942. It enabled every part of a motor to be given a thorough check before it was installed in one of the *Luftwaffe*'s aircraft. The radiator can be seen on the side of the test bed.

Below: Besides the Ju 188As and Es operated by 4/KG 66, II/KG 2 '*Holzhammer*' also flew Ju 188E-1 bombers in action during the summer of 1944. During Operation 'Steinbock' it operated some thirty-five E-1s, which were powered by BMW 801 MA radial engines. The upper surfaces of these aircraft were comprehensively camouflaged in order to provide as much protection as possible when flying over England. The type of bombs being carried indicate that the aircraft in the photograph was being used on a training mission, intended to familiarise a new crew with its workings.

Left: An elaborately-camouflaged Ju 188E (U5+EL) of 3/KG 2 flying to its front-line base during winter 1943–4. During the early months of 1944 several Ju 188s of the *'Holzhammer' Geschwader* were destroyed by British and American fighters, as the Allies attempted to demolish all German airfields and the very infrastructure of the *Luftwaffe* in preparation for the landings in Normandy that summer.

Left: Only a limited number of Me 410s were involved in raids against targets in England. Most of the Me 410 B-1s were operated by KG 2. They were equipped with a Stuvi 5B bomb sight. The bomb-bay could hold up to eight SC 50 bombs, two SC 250s, or two SC 500s. Because of its poor operational performance the Me 410 only replaced some of KG 2's Do 217s.

Left: The Me 410 was armed with four fixed guns in the nose section and two remote-controlled MG 131s in FSDL 131 side-fuselage barbettes of the same sort as those used in the Me 210. However, this armament proved too weak to be an efficient defence against marauding nightfighters.

Above: II/KG 40 sustained its offensive campaign in the face of overwhelming opposition mounted by British Coastal Command and the Royal Air Force. This He 177A-5 (KM+UJ, s/n 550 060) is being prepared for its next action over the Bay of Biscay. All upper surfaces are camouflaged in a pattern specifically designed for aircraft operating over water. The He 177A 5s of II/KG 40 flew their missions carrying remote-controlled glider bombs.

Below: This He 177A-3 has just landed on the runway at Munich-Riem airport in Bavaria, which was operated by the *Luftwaffe* during the Second World War. It was at Munich-Riem that the surviving A-3s were eventually decommissioned and scrapped, the paired DB 605s which went to make up their DB 610 engines being re-used, individually, to power Bf 109 fighter aircraft during the final stages of the war.

Left: Heavy Allied bombing raids against *Luftwaffe* installations and airfields took place all over France, Belgium and the Netherlands. This fin belongs to a damaged He 177A-5 bomber of I/KG 100 'Wiking' which was captured by American ground forces during September 1944. It belonged to 3 *Staffel*, and carried the code 6N+WL.

Right: A formation of I/KG 66 Ju 188s moves from one base to another early in 1944. In combat these aircraft carried SC 500 and BC 50 bombs along with large bomb containers (AB 500 and 1000) filled with small anti-personnel or anti-tank bomblets capable of inflicting severe losses on ground forces, especially when the latter were surprised whilst marching along a road with no available cover.

Below: A Ju 188E-1 of II/KG 2 '*Holzhammer*', which had received the first such aircraft during the winter of 1943—4. These more powerful bombers replaced the Do 217s which had formerly been used by II *Gruppe*. Lack of fuel and Allied air superiority made the surviving crews' missions very dangerous and costly.

Above: Crewmen of II/KG 2's 7 *Staffel* take a cup of *Ersatz* coffee after readying their Do 217M-1 (U5+DR) for action. The M-1 was armed with three MG 131s and two additional MG 15s. The seated men include Kurt Winkler and Frank Schumacher. The photograph was possibly taken on the *Luftwaffe* base at Coulommiers in northern France.

Left: A close-up view of one of the SC 1700 bombs with AZ 28 B/6 fuses which were widely used against British targets between 1941 and 1943. The SC 1700 had a total weight of 1,704 kg, a length of 3.3 m and a diameter of 0.66 m. It could pierce 60 mm armour plates without any difficulty. Note the damage to one segment of the bomb's tail. Despite the SC 1700's considerable weight, the lifting trolley facilitated the attachment of such large bombs beneath an aircraft's wing centre section without undue difficulty.

Right: The nose section of a Ju 188E-1 belonging to I/KG 66. Utilising its Ju 188E-1s along with several Ju 88S-1s and S-3s, KG 66 was deeply involved in Operation 'Steinbock'. At the time of these missions (early 1944) I *Gruppe* could operate a total of forty-five aircraft, including twenty-three serviceable Ju 88s and Ju 188s. The aircraft shown was sometimes flown by *Leutnant* Hans Altrogge, who lost his life on 15 April 1944 when piloting the second Do 335 prototype, which crashed near Memmingen in Bavaria.

Below: This Do 217M-1 (s/n 722753) of 7/KG 2 '*Holzhammer*' was photographed at Coulommiers in summer 1943. The aircraft was fitted with a FuG 216 Neptun R radar which warned the crew of the approach of enemy nightfighters. Despite this additional warning system and flame dampers, this aircraft was shot down by the crew of a De Havilland Mosquito on 15 August 1943.

Right: The *Abwurf-behälter* (weapons container, usually abbreviated to AB) was a method of bomb delivery widely employed by the *Luftwaffe*. The wooden AB 1000-2 contained 610 B1 incendiary bomblets with a total weight of 955 kg. Alternatively it could be used to house 238 B1EZ and 248 B2EZ incendiary bomblets, when its weight increased to some 960 kg. During raids these bomblets were used alongside SC 1000 or SC 1800 bombs fitted with fuses set to go off minutes, hours or even days after they had been dropped.

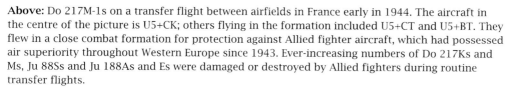

Above: Do 217M-1s on a transfer flight between airfields in France early in 1944. The aircraft in the centre of the picture is U5+CK; others flying in the formation included U5+CT and U5+BT. They flew in a close combat formation for protection against Allied fighter aircraft, which had possessed air superiority throughout Western Europe since 1943. Ever-increasing numbers of Do 217Ks and Ms, Ju 88Ss and Ju 188As and Es were damaged or destroyed by Allied fighters during routine transfer flights.

Above: This Do 217M-1 night bomber (U5+UK, s/n 722 125) belonging to 2/KG 2 is being prepared to participate in one of the 'Steinbock' raids mounted early in 1944. It is fitted with large flame damper tubes alongside the DB 603 A-1 piston engines. Defensive armament was often reduced to three MG 131s in order to save weight and make the aircraft faster. An AB 1000, filled with hundreds of small incendiary bomblets, stands in the foreground ready to be loaded.

Left: Only a few Do 217E-4s such as this were operated by II/KG 6, being used for offensive operations until spring 1943. This well-camouflaged pathfinder bomber, with most of its defensive armament missing, was possibly used for liaison duties. Units located in Western Europe customarily used one or two Do 217Es or Ks to cater for their transportation needs.

Above: One of the huge He 177A-3s is here shown being towed by a SdKfz 7, popularly known as an *8to-Zugmaschine* (eight-ton tractor). The photograph was taken at Châteaudun in France during the preparations for Operation 'Steinbock'. One member of the crew, decorated with an Iron Cross first class, supervises the hitching up of the aircraft behind its heavy tow-truck.

Above: KG 100's attack on London early in 1944 was carried out from Rheine. After dropping their bombs the unit's He 177s headed for Boulogne in France before returning to Rheine. Subsequent raids were launched from Châteaudun, from where London, Portsmouth, Bristol, Hull and Plymouth were all bombed. Nine He 177As were written off during these attacks, and four more were damaged. Most of these bombers belonged to the A-3 series, very few A-5s ever being shot down.

Left: The rear gunner of a He 177A-3 of 2 *Staffel* of KG 100 '*Wiking*' manoeuvres himself into his cramped fighting compartment, which, along with the size of his heavy MG 151/20 gun, allowed him very little freedom of movement. This aircraft (6N+SK) had the name 'Susy' painted in white beneath the forward cabin section.

Above: This He 177A-5 (6N+HN) belonged to 5 *Staffel* of II/KG 100 '*Wiking*', which since 5 May 1944 had been commanded by *Hauptmann* Bodo Mayerhofer. The aircraft has received the standard camouflage of black lower and dappled light grey upper surfaces.

Below: One of the Fieseler Fi 103 A-1 'V1' flying bombs — nicknamed 'Buzz bombs' by the English and *Höllenhunde*

(Hellhounds) by the Germans — which were fired against Southern England, and especially London, from launch sites in Western Europe manned by Flak-Regiment 155 (W), commanded by *Oberstleutnant* Max Wachtel. The first V1-equipped formations were activated at Zinnowitz and Zempin near Peenemünde. The loss of launch sites to enemy ground forces and air raids eventually led to V1s being launched from the air instead, using He 111 aircraft.

Above: A close-up of a V1-carrying He 111H-16 (A1+HK, s/n 161600) belonging to 2/KG 53, based at Ahlhorn. KG 53 operated some eighty Heinkel bombers capable of carrying 'Buzz bombs' suspended beneath the starboard wing root, and between them these launched some 300 V1s between July and August 1944 alone. Their last such mission was undertaken on 14 January 1945. Because these missions were carried out by night, the He 111's defensive armament was reduced.

Below: As a result of years of unsustainable losses suffered by *Luftwaffe* raiders flying against Britain, only robot bombs and missiles were employed against British targets after Operation 'Steinbock' ended in early 1944. This photograph shows a 'Buzz bomb' being fitted beneath a He 111H-16, of which as many as 105 were rebuilt to carry such missiles. A few He 111H-20s serving with KG 3 and KG 53 in 1944 and 1945 were also used to carry V1s. Early in 1945, however, a shortage of fuel terminated the combat operations of both units.

Wild Animals

OF NORTH AMERICA

A POSTER BOOK

Text by **Karl Meyer**

Have You Heard the Call of the Wild?

No matter where you live, wild animals are nearby. Some live in the city. Others live in the country. Some are easy to see, while others keep hidden. Owls pounce on mice. Bats snap up mosquitoes in the night sky. Beavers make ponds that other creatures share.

North America is a very big place and some of the animals in this book may live far away from you. People travel many miles to national parks to see animals that they can't see in their backyard. Visitors hike through woods and prairies to see a bison or spend days traveling on rivers to spot a bald eagle.

If we learn about wild animals and walk quietly where they live, we have a better chance of seeing and hearing them. Their wildness can feed our imaginations. Maybe you become quiet when you see a wild animal or find a strange track in mud or snow. That is the wildness inside of you — the part that keeps you wondering.

All animals add something special to our planet. Their work helps to keep the woods, fields, and rivers healthy. Learning about wild animals can help us to be better neighbors. Wild animals need places to live without roads or houses or noisy machines. And we all need wild places to share. Those places feed our spirits. Please take what you learn here, head outside, and go a little wild!

Caribou

• • • • • • • • • • • • • • • •

This caribou is rubbing off the blood-enriched layer of **velvet** (a soft covering) from its 4-foot antlers. Adult caribou grow and shed their antlers every year. The adult males shed their antlers by midwinter, after mating season is over. Though the male's antlers are larger, the female will keep hers until the long winter ends. The caribou is related to elk, moose, and deer.

At Home in the Wild

Caribou are creatures of cold northern **climates** (temperatures). They were once more widespread. Today just a small **herd** (group) remains in Idaho and Montana, but hundreds of thousands still live in Alaska and Canada. Caribou sometimes gather by the tens of thousands. Big herds follow the same routes year after year to find other caribou. They wear giant trails into the **tundra** (cold, soggy flatlands). Caribou are excellent swimmers and will cross wide rivers.

What's for Dinner?

Caribou feed on grasses, moss, willow leaves, twigs, and **lichens** (tough, chewy plants). Some caribou herds don't travel far, while others journey hundreds of miles between feeding areas. Wolves, lynx, bears, and humans hunt them. But a bigger problem is humans destroying their **habitat** (homes). People have caused caribou great harm by building roads, cutting forest, drilling for oil, and building giant dams where caribou live.

Did You Know?

A single calf is born in spring. It is able to walk within hours. New mothers and calves gather in groups called **nursery bands.** The **bulls** (males) grow up to weigh as much as 600 pounds.

Raccoon

. . . .

This young, masked creature is built to go anywhere. The raccoon's clawed, hand-like paws help it scamper up trees. Those paws also come in handy when it decides to swim or dive below the water in search of **prey** (animals being hunted). Raccoons cleverly use their paws to open trashcans and door latches in search of food.

At Home in the Wild

There's probably a raccoon near you right now. They live everywhere from southern Canada through Mexico. Raccoons live in forests, big cities, swamps, suburbs, and farmlands. The only places you won't find them are in the high, cold mountains. Raccoons do not **hibernate** (take a long winter sleep). In the coldest months, they stay warm and rest for several weeks in a hollow log, brush pile, burrow, or empty building.

What's for Dinner?

Raccoons eat everything! Mushrooms, snakes, grapes, corn, nuts, bugs, mice, eggs, birds, worms, clams, and human trash are on the raccoon's menu. Raccoons prefer living near water. They will dive in and snatch up crayfish in their paws or sneak up on resting frogs. Raccoons examine food carefully. They dunk it in water and appear to wash it with their paws. This helps them to find the best parts to eat.

Did You Know?

Raccoons give birth to 3 or 4 babies in summer. Babies are born blind and weigh just 2 ounces (about the weight of a candy bar). They will grow up to be nearly 3 feet long and weigh anywhere from 12 to 30 pounds.

photo © Denver Bryan/www.DenverBryan.com • *Wild Animals of North America*, Storey Publishing

Coyote

• • • • • • • • • • •

Coyotes are intelligent animals. Cartoons and legends always show them as smart tricksters. Coyotes are small enough to be quick and clever, but strong enough to bring down **prey** (animals being hunted). Adult coyotes weigh between 20 and 50 pounds. Coyotes are bigger than foxes and smaller than wolves.

At Home in the Wild

Before settlers killed off the wolves and chopped down forests in the eastern part of the country, coyotes lived only in the West. With the wolves gone, coyotes moved east into prairies, farmlands, open forests, river valleys, and suburbs. Today, coyotes live in every state but Hawaii. They even live in New York City and Los Angeles. Though rarely seen, coyotes give yips and high-pitched howls to signal their neighbors.

What's for Dinner?

Coyotes are active at night and usually hunt alone. They eat cottontail rabbits, hares, squirrels, snakes, frogs, birds, mice, bugs, acorns, and berries. Sometimes they gather in small **packs** (family groups). In this way they are sometimes able to bring down larger prey like young or injured deer. Wolves, bears, and cougars hunt coyotes, but humans are their main enemies. Coyotes are hunted for sport. They are also shot and poisoned because they sometimes kill farm animals.

Did You Know?

Healthy coyotes do not attack people. That is a **myth** (something that is often believed but is actually not true).

photo © Greg Lasley • *Wild Animals of North America*, Storey Publishing

Grizzly Bear

The salmon-catching grizzly bear is known as the brown bear in Alaska. Grizzlies are one of the largest land **carnivores** (meat eaters) in the world. Some grizzlies weigh over 800 pounds. Standing upright they can be 7 feet tall. The grizzly bear is related to the black bear and the polar bear. You can tell a grizzly bear by its large head and its brownish-yellow fur.

At Home in the Wild

Grizzly bears once roamed across most of western North America from Alaska into Mexico. Their only serious **predators** (hunters) were humans. In the 1800s, settlers moving west into grizzly bear **habitat** (homes) killed many bears to protect their livestock. Without large, wild territories to hunt and roam, grizzlies began to disappear. Today, they occupy just a tiny part of their former territory. Most live in the mountains and shrublands of Alaska and western Canada. Many live in **refuges** (safe places) and national parks.

What's for Dinner?

Grizzly bears eat lots of berries, roots, and grassy plants. They also kill elk, moose, and mountain sheep when they can. Some, like the one in this picture, also fatten up on salmon before they **hibernate** (take a long winter sleep). Grizzlies mostly avoid humans. But when humans surprise them or get between mothers and their cubs, they sometimes attack.

Did You Know?

In fall grizzlies scoop out **dens** (underground homes) on mountain slopes and beneath tree roots where they will hibernate during winter. Their winter hibernation can last up to 6 months.

photo © Harry Walker/AlaskaStock.com • *Wild Animals of North America*, Storey Publishing

Bald Eagle

I t's possible that these bald eagles are dancing in the air hundreds of feet up. Though competing eagles sometimes fight, males and females also lock **talons** (claws) in a breathtaking sky dance. This is part of their mating ritual. An adult bald eagle is 3 feet tall with a wingspan of over 7 feet. It can weigh more than 10 pounds.

At Home in the Wild

The bald eagle is our national symbol and a symbol of healthy rivers and woods. Bald eagles live along waterways throughout much of the United States, Canada, and Alaska. They once nearly disappeared from many parts of North America because they were being poisoned by chemicals and people were destroying their **habitat** (homes). Special laws were made to protect bald eagles and some deadly chemicals were banned. Those actions came just in time to save the eagles.

What's for Dinner?

Bald eagles eat rabbits, ducks, and sea birds, but they love fish. The bald eagle is also a **scavenger,** which means it often feeds on dead fish and animals. During fall, particularly in Alaska, bald eagles gather along rivers to feed on thousands of salmon. Though they are skilled at catching fish, bald eagles are also known for stealing. They will steal the live fish caught by a smaller hawk known as the osprey.

Did You Know?

Each spring bald eagles give birth to 2 or 3 **eaglets** (baby eagles) high in a stick-built nest that can weigh 2,000 pounds. The eaglets will be flying by midsummer, but it will be 5 years before they start nests of their own.

photo © Steve Bloom/stevebloom.com • *Wild Animals of North America,* Storey Publishing

Red Fox

• • • • • • • • • • • • • • • •

This red fox is **mousing** (hunting for mice). It is using its excellent hearing, sight, and smell to pounce on small **mammals** (warm-blooded animals) beneath the snow. Red foxes are **canines** (wild dogs) and are related to gray and Arctic foxes, coyotes, and wolves.

At Home in the Wild

Red foxes live almost anywhere but deserts and deep forests. They are found from the snowy Arctic to the farmlands, woods, and suburbs of Texas and Florida. Red foxes sleep outside during the winter. They ball up in the snow with their tails tucked around their noses for warmth. Female foxes give birth to their babies in **dens** (underground homes) in the spring. The dens are made of tunnels that can be up to 25 feet long. The dens usually face south to be warmed by the spring sun.

What's for Dinner?

Foxes eat various small mammals. They trap mice and **voles** (small animals related to mice and rats) with the same skill as housecats. They hunt frogs, squirrels, snakes, bugs, and rabbits. They also eat nuts, berries, grasses, corn, and fruit. Humans hunt foxes. Coyotes, wolves, bobcats, and lynx eat them.

Did You Know?

In spring, 4 or 5 **pups** (baby foxes) are born in a den. The pups weigh just a few ounces, but at five weeks old, they can walk to the den entrance. There, they will play-hunt with the bones and feathers their parents bring them. By fall, they will be fully grown.

Harbor Seal

• •

This harbor seal is taking a rest while the tide is out. It may look stranded, but it's just waiting for the tide to return. Harbor seals come out of the water onto rocks, sand, or ice to rest and be warmed by the sun. They sometimes gather in loose **colonies** (groups) of 100 or more.

At Home in the Wild

Harbor seals are one of the most common seals of the North American coasts. They live in both Atlantic and Pacific waters from northernmost Alaska and Canada down to California and the Carolinas. They can be found along sandy beaches, rocky coasts, harbors, and bays. They sometimes swim many miles upstream in rivers and lakes to catch fish.

What's for Dinner?

Harbor seals love to eat fish. Herring, flounder, cod, **smelt** (small silver-colored fish), and salmon make up part of their diet. They also eat squid, clams, shrimp, snails, and octopuses. They can easily chase down fleeing fish by quickly pumping their tails and steering with their flippers. Harbor seals can dive to over 500 feet and stay underwater for more than 20 minutes at a time.

Polar bears, sharks, **orcas** (killer whales), walruses, and humans hunt harbor seals. Humans sometimes kill harbor seals by accident when the seals get tangled in fishing nets.

Did You Know?

A single **pup** (baby seal) is born near water in spring or early summer. It weighs about 20 pounds.

Mountain Lion

• •

Mountain lions can pounce on **prey** (animals being hunted) from 20 feet away. They are swift hunters, able to outrun deer for short distances. Mountain lions are 6 to 9 feet long from the tip of the nose to the end of the tail. Large males can weigh up to 275 pounds. Their 4-toed prints are about the size of an adult's fist.

At Home in the Wild

Mountain lions (also called **cougars, panthers,** or **pumas**) live in mountains, swamps, and valleys from Canada to Mexico. Mountain lions once roamed woodlands and hills in the East. Humans shot most of them, and poisoned others. The woods that mountain lions needed for food and shelter were turned into farms. Today, mountain lions are extinct in most eastern lands, though a few Florida panthers still survive in the Everglades.

What's for Dinner?

Mountain lions hunt alone in wild areas for deer, elk, and moose. They kill big animals with their strong jaws and slashing claws. Mountain lions can't eat a whole deer at once so they cover the leftovers with leaves and dirt. They return later for their food. Mountain lions also eat rabbits, mice, squirrels, raccoons, beavers, and even porcupines. They will kill cows and have attacked people. Man is the mountain lion's main **predator** (hunter).

Did You Know?

The mother gives birth to 3 or 4 small **kittens** (baby mountain lions) in a cave, **crevice** (narrow opening in a rock), or brushy site. For the next 2 years, she will teach the kittens to hunt for themselves.

photo © Bret Hicken/Natural Exposures • *Wild Animals of North America,* Storey Publishing

White-Tailed Deer

This white-tailed deer **fawn** (young deer) looks like it's all tears. White-tailed deer have terrific hearing. They also see well and have an excellent sense of smell. This fawn waits in tall grass for its mother to come and nurse it. Its white spots are meant to look like patches of sun on the ground to fool **predators** (hunters).

At Home in the Wild

White-tailed deer are found in every region from southern Canada to Mexico except the dry Southwest. They live in forests, swamps, farm country, prairies, and brush lands.

What's for Dinner?

White-tailed deer eat a wide variety of vegetable matter. In spring and summer, they nibble grasses, berries, leaves, fruits, mushrooms, and corn. In fall, they also feed on the same nuts and acorns as the squirrels. In winter, they **browse** (eat the leaves of) twigs of low shrubs and trees and chew buds and needles of evergreens. Wolves, coyotes, lynx, bobcats, cougars, and unleashed, free-roaming dogs all kill deer, but humans are their biggest predators. At one time, white-tailed deer were almost lost in the East and Midwest from too much hunting. Today, they are common because many of their predators, including cougars and wolves, have been killed off.

Did You Know?

The **doe** (female) gives birth to 1 or 2 fawns in spring. The fawns have no scent. This helps to keep predators from finding them. Fully grown does weigh between 100 and 250 pounds. **Bucks** (males) are heavier and grow antlers that fall off each winter.

photo © robertmccaw.com • *Wild Animals of North America*, Storey Publishing

Humpback Whale

Imagine a bus shooting out of the ocean and landing with a huge splash. That's something like what happens when a humpback whale jumps completely out of the water, except a humpback is even *bigger* than a bus and weighs over 50,000 pounds! Its flippers are 25 feet long and make quite a splash when they hit the surface of the water. Humpbacks will **sound** (dive under) for up to 30 minutes. They also rest like logs near the surface.

At Home in the Wild

Humpback whales live, feed, and **migrate** (travel) off both the Atlantic and Pacific coasts. Humpbacks are **endangered** (very few left alive) worldwide. For hundreds of years, they were hunted for their bone and **blubber** (fat that is made into oil and used in lamps and other objects). Today, laws protect them from being hunted, but they are still killed or injured by giant fishing nets, boat crashes, and pollution. The **sonar** (sound waves) used by submarines may also be hurting them. Humpbacks communicate in the ocean using sound.

What's for Dinner?

Humpbacks capture small ocean creatures and schooling fish by gulping large amounts of water into their stretchy throats. They then push the water out through hundreds of filtering plates called **baleen** until only their **prey** (animals being hunted) remain. Sharks and **orcas** (killer whales) hunt humpback whales.

Did You Know?

Every other year a **cow** (female) will give birth to a single **calf** (baby whale) after traveling to tropical waters. A calf can weigh 4,000 pounds!

Bison

• • • • • • • • • • •

Bison, also called buffalo, are the largest land **mammals** (warm-blooded animals) in North America. **Bulls** (males) weigh over 2,000 pounds. They can run 30 miles an hour. Bison are excellent swimmers and have even crossed America's largest rivers.

At Home in the Wild

Just 400 years ago, 60 million bison lived in North America. They once roamed from Alaska to Florida and across the Great Plains to Mexico. They **migrated** (traveled) in large **herds** (groups) of 100,000 or more. But European settlers moving west slaughtered millions of bison. By 1900 only a few hundred bison remained.

At that time a small, wild herd was living in the area of today's Yellowstone National Park. Concerned citizens made President Theodore Roosevelt aware that the bison would soon disappear completely. New laws were passed stopping all bison hunting. Yellowstone National Park and other **refuges** (safe places) were created where bison and other wild animals could roam wild and free. Today, about 250,000 bison roam grasslands and open woods.

What's for Dinner?

Bison eat grasses and other short plants. Grizzly bears, cougars, and wolves hunt them. Native Americans hunted bison for food. They made tee-pees, clothes, blankets, and tools from the hides and bone. People still eat bison today and many farms raise bison for meat.

Did You Know?

Each spring, a single **calf** (baby bison) is born. It can stand in just 30 minutes and run in just hours.

Gray Wolf

This gray wolf is playing with its food! Gray wolves live in **packs** (family groups) and will hunt large **prey** (animals being hunted). But even though these wild **canines** (dogs) often weigh more than 100 pounds, they are happy with small snacks, too. The word *canine* comes from the sharp teeth these **predators** (hunters) use to grab their prey. The gray wolf is related to the fox, the coyote, and even the domestic dog.

At Home in the Wild

Five hundred years ago, wolves roamed all of North America. They hunted in mountains, rivers, woods, and prairies. When Europeans arrived here, they feared wolves. They saw wolves as competitors and a threat to farm animals. They shot and poisoned wolves, cut down forests, and fenced the prairies where wolves hunted. Within 400 years, wolves disappeared from almost every state but Alaska. But today, government programs are helping wolves return to Idaho, Montana, Arizona, and North Carolina.

What's for Dinner?

Working in teams, wolf packs can chase, ambush, and kill animals larger than themselves. Deer, moose, elk, bison, and caribou are some of their larger prey. But they also eat smaller prey, including mice, beavers, rabbits, birds, fish, squirrels, and bugs. Meat isn't everything. In summer, wolves eat fruit, berries, nuts, and grasses.

Did You Know?

Wolves do not attack people. That is a **myth** (something that is often believed but is actually not true). They see us as *their* predators. The howls they give are to proclaim their **territory**.

Moose

• • • • • • • • • • • • •

The antlers on this **bull** (male) moose are still growing. They are covered in a soft layer called **velvet.** It will be rubbed off when the antlers stop growing in late summer. Only the bulls have antlers, which fall off every year. Bulls competing for the attention of a nearby **cow** (female) moose may shove each other with their antlers. Very rarely, their antlers lock together and can't be separated. If that happens, the bulls **starve** (die from hunger).

At Home in the Wild

Moose live in northern evergreen forests and also in some leafy woodlands. They feed along rivers, ponds, bogs, meadows, and lakes. Moose are found from Alaska and Canada south into the northern states. They are good swimmers. They will dunk themselves in ponds or sink themselves in mud to escape biting flies. Moose also travel to places called **salt licks** (smooth, rocky surfaces where salt and other minerals are lapped up by visiting animals).

What's for Dinner?

Moose eat tree bark and twigs, **lichens** (tough, chewy plants), moss, pondweeds, grasses, mushrooms, and flowering plants. In summer, moose will dive underwater in lakes and bogs to reach plants rich in nutrients and salt. Wolves, cougars, bears, and humans hunt moose. A cow moose's call sounds something like a dairy cow's. Hunters imitate this call to trick bulls into coming close to them.

Did You Know?

A cow gives birth to one or two 20-pound **calves** (baby moose) in late spring. Mothers sometimes swim to islands to give birth where calves are safe from **predators** (hunters).

Diamondback Rattlesnake

This Western diamondback rattlesnake has some fancy equipment. Its fangs are hidden on the roof of its mouth. They'll swing forward when the snake strikes at an animal. The openings in front of the eyes are called **pits.** The pits sense heat so the diamondback can locate warm prey in the dark. The dry rattles at the end of its tail shake loudly to warn predators to stay away.

At Home in the Wild

Western diamondbacks are found from southern California to Texas and Arkansas. They live not only in dry, rocky places, but also in grasslands, sandy coastal areas, and brushy woods. Western diamondbacks use the sun and earth to keep warm. They gather in warm **dens** (underground homes) to keep from freezing in winter.

What's for Dinner?

Western diamondbacks hunt mice, birds, and even squirrels, rabbits, and prairie dogs. They inject **venom** (poison) that soon **paralyzes** (stuns) their prey. They follow injured animals partly by smelling with their tongues. A rattlesnake's jaws stretch wide to swallow bigger prey. Hawks, owls, and roadrunners hunt western diamondbacks.

Did You Know?

Western diamondbacks are usually 3 to 5 feet long, but some grow to be more than 6 feet. Western diamondbacks **molt** (shed their skin) at least once a year. A new rattle segment is added each time the snake sheds its skin. Rattles can wear off or be broken off.

photo © agefotostock/SuperStock • *Wild Animals of North America,* Storey Publishing

Wild Horses

●●●●●●●●●●●●●●●●●●●●●●●

These wild horses are trotting along the Virginia–Maryland coast. Bigger **herds** (groups) of wild horses live on **refuges** (safe places) in many western states. **Fossils** (imprints of old bones) of the earliest horses — tiny creatures just 3 feet tall — have been found in North America. Larger, single-toed horses, like those of today, lived here 2 million years ago. But then they disappeared suddenly, thousands of years ago. Scientists think the changing **climate** (temperature) may have killed them. Others believe human Ice Age hunters caused them to disappear.

At Home in the Wild

The free-roaming wild horses of today returned to North America in the 1500s when Spanish explorers brought tame horses here. Some were abandoned and survived on their own in the wild. The Plains Indians captured and re-tamed some. They used them in bison hunts. Today's wild herds came from tame horses that were left to go wild. Wild horses live on refuges in Maryland, Virginia, Nevada, Wyoming, Colorado, California, Oregon, and Utah.

What's for Dinner?

Wild horses graze **scrublands** (areas of small trees and shrubs), coasts, and grassy plains. They eat grasses, grasslike plants, and also **browse** (eat the leaves of) shrubs. Some people bring in farm hay to make sure the wild herds have enough to eat.

Did You Know?

The fossils of some of the world's oldest known horses show that they were the size of small dogs and had four toes on each front foot.

photo © Allison Turner, National Park Service • *Wild Animals of North America,* Storey Publishing

Elk

• • • • • • •

This **bull** (male) elk may weigh 1,000 pounds! Its antlers may be 5 feet long and weigh 30 pounds each. Bulls have 6 **tines** (points) on each antler, so they need thick necks to carry those heavy racks. **Cows** (females) don't grow antlers. The elk is also known by its Native American name, Wapiti.

At Home in the Wild

Elk live in grasslands, high valleys, and woods from Canada to Texas. They once spread out all the way to the East Coast, but then settlers moved west over a hundred years ago and killed them off. Very few elk remained after that.

Laws were passed to protect the remaining **herds** (groups). **Refuges** (safe places) and national parks were set up for elk and other creatures. Some elk were protected on Native American lands. Today, almost 1 million elk live in the wild.

What's for Dinner?

Elk eat grasses and low grassy plants. They also **browse** (eat the leaves of) shrubs and strip the bark from trees and twigs. Mountain lions and wolves eat elk. Bears, coyotes, bobcats, and other **predators** (hunters) kill young elk. Humans hunt elk for food and for their antlers.

Did You Know?

Bull elk **bugle** (make a loud noise) during mating season to help attract cows. The bugling starts out low and deep and ends in a high whistle. Bulls sometimes fight over cows. They go head-to-head with their antlers.

Snowshoe Hare

Bigfoot would be a good name for the snowshoe hare. Its large hind feet help it to sprint 30 miles an hour on top of the snow. It can jump 12 feet in a single leap! Snowshoe hares are also called **varying hares,** because the color of their fur changes to blend in with the land. In winter, a snowshoe hare's fur is white like the snow, while in summer its color changes to gray-brown to match the earth. These color changes, called **camouflage,** hide it from **predators** (hunters).

At Home in the Wild

Snowshoe hares live in northern forests across Alaska and Canada, and south into the colder forests and mountains of the northern states. They are found in dense evergreen forests, swamps, and thickets. They also live in areas of mixed evergreens and leafy woods. Snowshoe hares are only found in areas with snowy winters.

What's for Dinner?

In spring, summer, and fall, snowshoe hares nibble berries, grasses, clover, and other leafy vegetation. When winter arrives, they feed on bark and twigs of willow and aspen trees, plus various shrubs and evergreen buds. Many creatures, including humans, hunt snowshoe hares. Owls and hawks eat them, and so do wolves, coyotes, **fishers** (weasel-like animals), foxes, and bobcats.

Did You Know?

Snowshoe hares give birth to 2, 3, or 4 babies, sometimes 3 times a year. The young are called **leverets.**

photo © robertmccaw.com • *Wild Animals of North America,* Storey Publishing

Polar Bears

● ● ● ● ● ● ● ● ● ● ● ● ● ● ● ● ● ● ●

Dancing bears? No, these polar bears are probably fighting over food or land. In the springtime, males sometimes fight over females. Polar bears can weigh 1,000 pounds or more! They are bigger than grizzly or black bears. A polar bear can stand 10 feet tall.

At Home in the Wild

Polar bears live along frozen coasts, islands, and sea ice of northern Alaska, Canada, and the Hudson Bay. Polar bears and native Inuit people have shared this snowy territory for 10,000 years. Long legs and wide, furred paws help these bears to swim. They have been spotted swimming miles from the nearest ice or land. Today, more humans are moving into their areas in search of oil, gas, and minerals. But a much bigger problem for the polar bears may be **global warming** (warmer temperatures all over the earth). The ice they depend on for seal hunting is slowly disappearing.

What's for Dinner?

On the sea ice, polar bears hunt ringed seals, catching them with sharp claws when the seals surface. They capture young walruses and harp seals, too. In summer, they travel the rocky edges of bays, gobbling up mosses, crabs, mussels, and bird's eggs. Polar bears also feed on the **blubber** (fat) of whales that wash ashore.

Did You Know?

The polar bears' coats have special hollow hairs that capture and hold the sun's warmth to keep them from getting cold. And their skin is actually black, which helps them to absorb heat from the sun.

Dall's Sheep

These male Dall's sheep are testing each other's strength. **Rams** (males) can weigh 200 pounds, while **ewes** (females) weigh about 125 pounds. This shoving match is the quiet part. At times, adult rams rear-up on their hind legs and charge each other at full speed from 15 feet away. Winners of these battles have a better chance of mating with the ewes.

At Home in the Wild

Dall's sheep live in cold northern mountains. They **graze** (find food) on rocky ridges, in tight valleys, and in high meadows from Alaska to British Columbia. Their tough, flexible hooves help them to balance and move quickly in the rocky areas where they travel above the **tree line** (an area where trees can't grow). Living in the high mountains helps to keep them safe from **predators** (hunters). Dall's sheep **migrate** (travel) in **herds** (groups) to lower pastures in spring to graze on tender young plants.

What's for Dinner?

In winter, Dall's sheep eat shrubs, moss, and dry grasses on wind-swept ledges. They will travel far to find places called **salt licks** in spring. Salt licks are smooth, rocky surfaces where salt and other minerals are lapped up by visiting animals. They nibble grasses and tender greens all summer and fall. Wolves, wolverines, lynx, coyotes, grizzly bears, and golden eagles hunt Dall's sheep. Humans shoot them to display their large horns.

Did You Know?

Dall's sheep are 4 to 5 feet long. Darker-colored bighorn sheep that live farther to the south are their close relatives.

photo © Ronald S. Phillips/AlaskaStock.com • *Wild Animals of North America*, Storey Publishing

Pronghorn

The pronghorn is one of a kind. It has no other relatives in North America. Its wide-set eyes help it to spot far-off danger. When danger is near, it displays a circle of bright hairs on its **rump** (rear end) to the **herd** (group). This signals the herd to run. The pronghorn is one of the fastest **mammals** (warm-blooded animals) on earth. Its thick chest helps it gulp air for running.

At Home in the Wild

Pronghorns live on open western plains, prairies, and desert valleys from southern Canada to Mexico. Pronghorns are fast. A herd may sprint away at 60 miles an hour! Before European settlers moved west, pronghorns roamed the same prairies as bison. There were tens of millions of pronghorns. But settlers killed them, along with the bison. The barbed wire fences put up for cattle also injured them. When the killing ended, the pronghorn herds were tiny. New laws were made to protect them, and they began to recover. Today, over a half million live in the West.

What's for Dinner?

Pronghorns nibble grasses and weeds and **browse** (eat the leaves of) woody shrubs and cactuses. Wolves, bobcats, coyotes, and bears eat pronghorns. Humans hunt them, too.

Did You Know?

Each spring **twins** (2 babies) are born. The mother hides each one in a separate place to help fool **predators** (hunters). She stays close by and visits to nurse them.

photo © dean-pearson.com • *Wild Animals of North America*, Storey Publishing

Nine-Banded Armadillo

• • • • • • • • • • • • • • • • •

This bony-plated creature is the only member of the armadillo family living in North America. Nine-banded armadillos are about 3 feet long from the tip of the head to the tip of the tail. They arrived in North America in just the last 200 years. Nine-banded armadillos walked here from Mexico and South America.

At Home in the Wild

Nine-banded armadillos live across the southeastern United States. They are found from Texas and Oklahoma to Florida in areas with woods or shrubs. They need to have water nearby all year long and soil they can dig in. If an armadillo needs to cross a small stream, it may walk underwater across the bottom. If the stream is large, it will sometimes suck in air and inflate its stomach like a life raft and paddle across. Armadillos are great diggers. An armadillo **den** (underground home) may have many entrances and tunnels 20 feet long.

What's for Dinner?

With **snouts** (noses) like anteaters, nine-banded armadillos sniff up worms, ants, spiders, mites, berries, crayfish, and bird eggs. Humans hunt armadillos and sometimes dislike them for digging in lawns, but they may actually be helping by gobbling up unwanted critters.

Did You Know?

Each spring an armadillo will give birth to 4 identical babies, either 4 males or 4 females, from a single egg. This is one reason why scientists study this **unique** (one-of-a-kind) creature.

American Alligator

The fierce-looking American alligator is North America's largest **reptile** (cold-blooded animal). It can grow to be 15 feet long, and it can weigh up to 1,000 pounds! Most American alligators are 8 to 10 feet long.

At Home in the Wild

Alligators live in the South from Texas and Oklahoma to North Carolina. They live near the coast in marshes and canals. Farther inland, they live on freshwater rivers, in lakes, and in swamps. At one time, humans killed so many alligators to make boots and clothes from their hides that alligators nearly became **extinct** (lost forever). Laws against hunting alligators have helped to protect the American alligator, and the number of alligators is growing in some areas.

What's for Dinner?

Alligators live on any type of prey that they can fit in their mouths, such as fish, reptiles, and birds. They hunt by lying quietly at the surface of the water and waiting for prey to float by, or they swim underwater and then pounce. Alligators can run for short distances and sometimes catch deer on land. Raccoons, bears, large birds, and turtles may eat alligator eggs and tiny young, but only humans hunt adult alligators.

Did You Know?

Females build large nests of mud and weeds. Nests can be 10 feet wide and 3 feet tall and contain 25 to 60 eggs.

photo © Brian Jorg/Critter Zone • *Wild Animals of North America*, Storey Publishing

Bobcat

• • • • • • • • • • • • • •

This bobcat looks like it's about to jump. Bobcats don't like to run far. They prefer to dash and pounce. They have powerful legs, sharp claws, and keen eyesight to help them hunt. The bobcat gets its name from its stubby, bobbed tail, which is black on top and white below. It is related to the jaguar, cougar, and lynx.

At Home in the Wild

Bobcats live in woods, mountains, swamps, deserts, bogs, and brushy areas from southern Canada to Florida and Mexico. They like areas with rocky places nearby. Bobcats are excellent climbers. They won't live in places that don't have any trees. Bobcats use trees to escape **predators** (hunters), to rest, and to ambush larger **prey** (animals being hunted). Bobcats dislike water, but they do swim.

What's for Dinner?

Bobcats are truly **carnivores** (meat eaters). Vegetables and fruits do not interest these cats at all. Bobcats hunt mostly at night. They pounce on rabbits, squirrels, snakes, birds, hares, and mice. Bobcats will make surprise attacks on young deer from the branches of trees. They hide in trees or among rocks when they see predators approaching. Their predators include coyotes, cougars, wolves, dogs, and humans.

Did You Know?

In spring, 1 to 4 blind, helpless **kittens** (baby bobcats) are born on a grass-lined ledge, cave, or hollow log. The mother provides all of their care and teaches them to hunt. Kittens stay with the mother into their first winter.

photo © agefotostock/SuperStock • *Wild Animals of North America*, Storey Publishing

California Leaf-Nosed Bat

• •

The California leaf-nosed bat is an excellent nighttime hunter. It sees **prey** (animals being hunted) well in the dark, and its large ears can track tiny sounds. Like other kinds of bats, California leaf-nosed bats find their prey by using sounds. They send out high-pitched sounds that **echo** (bounce) off nearby prey. The sounds return to the bats' ears, telling them where to fly. The bat's name comes from a small, leafy-looking, triangular flap above its nose.

At Home in the Wild

California leaf-nosed bats live in dry, rocky mountains and deserts from southern Nevada and California to Arizona and Mexico. They sleep upside down by day, hanging by their feet in mines, caves, and rock shelters. They may rest in **roosts** (groups) of up to 500 bats. Like many other kinds of bats, California leaf-nosed bats are disappearing. One reason is that curious humans enter the caves and mines where they roost and disturb them.

What's for Dinner?

California leaf-nosed bats eat a variety of moths, flying and crawling beetles, grasshoppers, **cicadas** (large, flying, plant-sucking insects), and other insects. They capture prey while flying. They can take off from the ground and often hover and pounce on crawling insects.

Did You Know?

In late spring, the mothers gather in separate groups when they are about to give birth. Females give birth while perching right side up.

Black Bear

• •

A black bear can weigh more than 2 adults combined. Still, most black bears will run for cover at the first sight of people. Black bears are excellent climbers. They will spread out branches to form a bed high off the forest floor. They are most active after sundown and before dawn.

At Home in the Wild

Black bears live in eastern and western states. They are at home in mountains, woodlands, and swamps. They also live in northern evergreen woods and marshy places from Alaska through much of Canada. Black bears prepare winter **dens** (underground homes) under brush piles, tree roots, or rocks and in caves or snow banks. They sleep in their dens and live off their body fat until spring. If disturbed, sleeping bears awaken quickly.

What's for Dinner?

Black bears eat mostly plants. They eat berries, bark, nuts, twigs, corn, fruit, and leaves. They also tear up stumps to gobble ants and insects and their eggs, and they sometimes eat small **mammals** (warm-blooded animals). They love honey. They are also attracted to bird feeders, human garbage dumps, and campsites if they smell food. Wolves, grizzly bears, and humans hunt black bears.

Did You Know?

January is the time **bear cub twins** (2 baby bears) or **triplets** (3 baby bears) are born. Black bear cubs weigh less than a pair of shoes! The **sow** (mother) nurses them in the warm den until spring.

photo © robertmccaw.com • *Wild Animals of North America*, Storey Publishing

Mountain Goat

• •

Even in summer, mountain goats linger near the snow. Their white coats, when seen against the snow, help to disguise them from **predators** (hunters). Mountain goats have tough hooves with flexible, pebbly inner pads that act almost like suction cups. These sure-footed animals climb over rocky heights that would make us dizzy. Mountain goats are the only members of the mountain antelope family living in North America.

At Home in the Wild

Mountain goats live in the mountains of Idaho, Montana, and Washington, and all the way up to southern Alaska. Mountain goats are tough and alert. With their specially adapted hooves, they can easily walk narrow, 6-inch-wide ledges that are hundreds of feet high. This mountain goat **grazes** (eats the grass of) a summer meadow in Glacier National Park. But its winter home might be just above the trees on the ledges and cliffs of the mountain in the background.

What's for Dinner?

In summer, mountain goats feed on grasses and wildflowers in mountain meadows. In the cold winter months, they nibble mosses and evergreen shoots that cling to high rocks. Their windy mountain homes and their amazing balance give them some safety from predators. Wolves, grizzlies, and mountain lions eat mountain goats. Humans hunt them for sport.

Did You Know?

Both **billies** (males) and **nannies** (females) have horns. The males' horns are longer than the females'. Counting the number of rings on the horns can tell you a mountain goat's age.

Black-Tailed Prairie Dog

• •

This black-tailed prairie dog is probably barking a message to its prairie dog neighbors. Black-tailed prairie dogs are a little over a foot tall. They live together in **prairie dog towns** (groups of prairie dogs). Sometimes thousands of prairie dogs will share a system of **burrows** (holes in the ground) and tunnels that can be 15 feet deep.

At Home in the Wild

Black-tailed prairie dogs live on flat and rolling **prairies** (grasslands) from southern Canada to Texas and Arizona. At one time, there were many more prairie dogs. Some prairie dog towns had millions of inhabitants! But when settlers moved west they brought along herds of cattle. To provide more grass for the cattle, ranchers began poisoning prairie dogs. The biggest prairie dog towns disappeared.

What's for Dinner?

Black-tailed prairie dogs feed on grasses and other short, leafy plants. They will hug, nuzzle, and greet each other and then feed together. They keep the grass well clipped around their towns. That short grass helps prairie dogs spot **predators** (hunters) including badgers, coyotes, rattlesnakes, hawks, and burrowing owls.

Did You Know?

Prairie dogs live in family groups called **coteries** with a single male, several adult females, and some younger prairie dogs. In spring, the adult females give birth to 3, 4, or 5 **pups** (prairie dog babies).

Western Screech Owl

The huge eyes of this western screech owl let in plenty of light for night hunting, which helps in catching **prey** (animals being hunted) like this snake. The feathers around the eyes help in hunting, too. They move tiny sounds toward the owl's hidden ears. And the western screech owl has special feathers that let it fly in silence. This allows it to make surprise attacks.

At Home in the Wild

Western screech owls live across much of western North America from southern Alaska to Texas. They live almost anywhere they can find sheltering trees and water, except for high in the mountains. They rest in the **cavities** (holes) of old trees by day. They use the deep, saw-dusty floors of woodpecker holes as nests.

What's for Dinner?

Western screech owls eat snakes, mice, fish, insects, birds, **shrews** (related to moles), and crayfish. They snatch prey with sharp **talons** (claws). Small creatures like mice are swallowed whole. Later, they cough up a dry **pellet** (small pebble-sized object) that is the leftover bones, fur, and feathers. Hawks, crows, raccoons, snakes, weasels, and larger owls eat screech owls.

Did You Know?

Western screech owls stay together for life. The female is larger than the male. She lays 2 to 5, small, white eggs and warms them around the clock. The male hunts and brings food to the nesting mother.

photo © Tom Vezo Wildlife Photography • *Wild Animals of North America*, Storey Publishing

Beaver

• • • • • • • • • • • •

This beaver is dragging both its food and its shelter. This is North America's largest **rodent** (gnawing mammal). Beavers have warm fur, webbed hind feet, and strong, flattened tails. Each one is over 3 feet long and can weigh more than 50 pounds. At one time, so many beavers were trapped to make fur coats and hats that they nearly disappeared. Today, laws protect them.

At Home in the Wild

Beavers live throughout North America in any place with trees and water. One beaver can cut down a 5-inch tree in just 15 minutes. They are natural engineers. Beavers carry branches and small logs to the water to build **dams** (walls that prevent water from flowing) and **lodges** (the beavers' dry, warm homes). They may eat the bark right away or store it underwater to eat later in the winter. Beaver dams can be short or hundreds of feet long. Big lodges may be 6 feet high and hold up to 12 related beavers. Lodges have underwater entrances for safety.

What's for Dinner?

In summer, beavers eat soft pond and river plants. They gobble the nutritious underwater roots, too. Bark is the beavers' main winter food. They store small branches under the mud near the lodge for winter eating. Foxes, coyotes, bobcats, wolves, otters, and **fishers** (animals related to weasels) eat beavers. Humans trap them.

Did You Know?

The mother gives birth to 2, 3, or 4 babies in the lodge in spring. They are called **kits.**

Midland Painted Turtles

• •

These midland painted turtles have found a place in the sun to rest. Midland painted turtles sometimes **bask** (rest in the sun) for hours to help their bodies stay at the right temperature. Basking also helps them to get important vitamins and to keep their shells free of disease. Each **carapace** (shell) of these turtles is 4 to 8 inches long.

At Home in the Wild

Midland painted turtles live in southern Quebec and down across the Midwest into Tennessee. They have many close relatives, including eastern, southern, and western painted turtles. As a group, painted turtles live all over much of the United States. Midland painted turtles live in ponds, slow rivers, and lakes. They need flat rocks and logs for basking. In the coldest months, they may bury themselves in mud at the water's bottom, absorbing oxygen through their skin.

What's for Dinner?

Midland painted turtles feed underwater on plants, insects, crayfish, snails, fish, and amphibian eggs. Herons, raccoons, foxes, frogs, skunks, and snakes eat young midland painted turtles and their eggs.

Did You Know?

Females migrate over land to dig nests in soft, sandy soil in spring or early summer. Females usually lay about 6 eggs in a nest but there can be up to 20 eggs. The turtles hatch in late summer and head toward water on their own.

The mission of Storey Publishing is to serve our customers
by publishing practical information that encourages
personal independence in harmony with the environment.

Edited by Sarah Guare
Art direction by Vicky Vaughn
Text design and production by Kristy MacWilliams
Cover photograph © agefotostock/SuperStock
Additional interior photographs © Greg Lasley, title page;
© Shattel/Rozinski, intro page; © Harry Walker/AlaskaStock.com, this page.

Printed in Hong Kong by Elegance Printing
10 9 8 7 6 5 4 3 2 1

Other Storey Titles You Will Enjoy

Eye See You: A Poster Book. Watch the watchers with 30 full-color, pull-out portraits of creatures with arresting gazes that tell fascinating stories. On the back are general facts about the animal and information about those amazing eyes. 64 pages. Paperback. ISBN 1-58017-643-7.

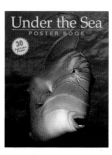

Under the Sea Poster Book. Bring the aquarium home with 30 full-color, pull-out portraits of fantastic sea creatures that kids love, plus all the fun facts that make each ocean resident unique and exciting. 64 pages. Paperback. ISBN 1-58017-623-2.

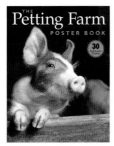

The Petting Farm Poster Book. Thirty pull-out posters feature beautifully reproduced full-color images of sweet chicks, ducklings, kids, lambs, calves, foals, piglets, rabbits, and more. The back of each poster contains fun facts about the animal's breed, habits, and history. 64 pages. Paperback. ISBN 1-58017-597-X.

Horses & Friends Poster Book. These 30 full-color posters feature horses with ponies, dogs, cats, goats, and other adorable companion animals. The irresistible posters are made for pulling out and decorating bedrooms, playrooms, lockers, or stables. 64 pages. Paperback. ISBN 1-58017-580-5.

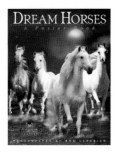

Dream Horses: A Poster Book. Celebrate the beauty, the power, and the majesty of horses with 30 full-color, large-format posters of horses in captivating, dreamlike scenes created by master photographer Bob Langrish. Inspiring text accompanies each fantastical poster. 64 pages. Paperback. ISBN 1-58017-547-0.

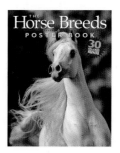

The Horse Breeds Poster Book. Suitable for hanging on bedroom walls, in school lockers, or even in barns, these 30 posters show horses in a range of sizes and colors, at work and in competition. Facts about the pictured horse breeds are included on the back of each poster. 64 pages. Paperback. ISBN 1-58017-507-4.

These and other books by Storey Publishing are available wherever quality books are sold or by calling 1-800-441-5700. Visit us at www.storey.com.